DOUBLE Your Money in SIX YEARS

How to Reap Profits in Discounted Mortgages

DOUBLE YOUR MONEY

by

D.
R
o
b
e
r
t

How to Reap Profits

PARKER PUBLISHING CO., INC.

IN SIX YEARS:

B
u
r
l
e
i
g
h

in Discounted Mortgages

WEST NYACK, NEW YORK

DOUBLE YOUR MONEY IN SIX YEARS
HOW TO REAP PROFITS IN DISCOUNTED MORTGAGES
BY
D. ROBERT BURLEIGH

© 1971, BY

PARKER PUBLISHING COMPANY, INC.
WEST NYACK, NEW YORK

LIBRARY OF CONGRESS
CATALOG CARD NUMBER: 70-158181

"This publication is designed to provide accurate and
authoritative information in regard to the subject
matter covered. It is sold with the understanding
that the publisher is not engaged in rendering legal,
accounting, or other professional service. If legal
advice or other expert assistance is required, the
services of a competent professional person should
be sought.

. . . From the Declaration of Principles jointly
adopted by a Committee of the American Bar Association and a Committee of Publishers and Associa-
tions."

PRINTED IN THE UNITED STATES OF AMERICA
ISBN 0-13-218818-x
B & P

TO

PHILLIP D. HEIB
A Dependable Guide

WHAT THIS BOOK WILL
DO FOR YOU

I shall start by telling you something you know very well, something so important that you spend a good deal of time thinking about it. *You want to make money.*

That desire produces four types of investment activity: (1) slow and steady accumulation, where the investor keeps adding to his savings accounts (with a concurrent increase in his life insurance reserves and his home equity); (2) intermittent investment, swinging back and forth between speculative ventures (which often produce more losses than profits) and the safety of savings deposits at low interest; (3) regular investment by a professional who knows how to earn a steady, high return; and (4) constant speculation, where the gambler shoots for high stakes—and usually loses most of the money he commits.

This is a book for all of the four types of investors I have listed because it provides the key to a field of investment that will produce varying yields, exactly proportionate to the degree of risk. *Within the range of safety, however, it will produce a yield that will double your money in six years.*

● DISCOUNTING IS THE KEY

A mortgage discounter takes a percentage of the amount owing on a mortgage as a fee for collecting that obligation at a later date. That fee might be as small as 1%. *Witness:* An acquaintance of mine paid $2,970 for a $3,000 first mortgage on a four-unit apartment building (valued at $40,000) that was to be paid off in $100 monthly installments, including 6% interest. (That investment should be safe enough to suit the most conservative saver.)

At the other end of the scale is a fee of approximately 50%. *Witness:* On December 30, 1970, I paid $2,000 for a $3,950 mortgage that was to be paid in $40 monthly installments, including 8% interest, until November 22, 1975, at which time the remaining balance must be paid. (The profitable nature of this discount operation, which virtually indicates an instantaneous doubling of my money, should satisfy the wildest speculator.)

Now that I have given these two contrasting examples—to prove that this book is for every investor—I shall concentrate on the middle range of discounts, which are sufficiently attractive to produce the return promised by the title, a doubling of your money in six years.

● HOW IT'S DONE

Here is a demonstration of that kind of profitable program of mortgage investments that is perfectly safe and proves the point:

Start with $1,600 and buy a $2,000 second mortgage that pays $20 a month, including 7% interest. (You can buy it at that price because it was offered at a standard discount of 20%.) After five years and ten months, you will have received $1,400 in installment payments. You will have deposited these monthly $20 sums in a savings account, paying 5% interest. In the five years and ten months, your interest on these deposits will amount to approximately $214. Add this to your $1,400 to make a total of $1,614. You withdraw $1,600 and buy another $2,000 mortgage.

Here is your financial statement:

The new mortgage...$2,000.00
Balance still due on original mortgage...........................1,284.00
Amount remaining in your savings account......................14.00
Your original $1,600 has now become.............................$3,298.00*

---

*If you deposit the same sum in a savings account paying 5% interest on a quarterly basis, it takes approximately 14 years to reach a balance of $3,200.

● I WILL BE YOUR GUIDE

Although this book is my personal story, with illustrations and examples drawn from my own experience, it is written in such a way that it can serve as a guide for your investments.

I have made it a point to assume that you know nothing about discounting and very little about mortgages. As we proceed, therefore, you will be led, step by step, into a specialized field of real estate investment that is extremely profitable.

Read the book for fun, if you like. Then go back, chapter by chapter, and study it carefully. You will then be ready to make your own investments—whether they be in discounted mortgages or real estate loans—with the knowledge that you can check back to a valuable guide as you investigate, negotiate, keep your books, prepare your income tax reports, and make your collections.

Plunge in! *Make money!*

ACKNOWLEDGMENTS

All the homeowners mentioned in this book are real people whose names have been changed. Except for a few examples which have been altered to demonstrate a particular point under discussion, the mortgage figures, rates of interest, and discount percentages are those of actual transactions. This is not the case with the financial statements in the chapter on bookkeeping. These statements, though based on my own operations, are fictitious.

I wish to extend special thanks to Phillip Heib and Harold Mayer for their assistance and encouragement in the period when I was still wondering if I could write this book.

For the additional material that transformed a short personal account into a worthwhile handbook, I wish to thank: Allan B. Polin; Leonard Williams, C.P.A.; Perry D. Caiopoulos, National Service Representative of the Pioneer National Title Insurance Company; Miss Fern Cheesebro, Executive Manager of the Apartment Association of Los Angeles County, Inc.; Leo Rodgers, Loan Service Representative, Veterans Administration; Gillespie Randolph, Deputy Commissioner, California Real Estate Commission; Miss Virginia Maroney, Escrow Officer, Security Pacific National Bank; Donald T. Anderson, Assistant Secretary, Title Insurance and Trust Company; and Morse Hazelrigg.

D.R.B.

CONTENTS

11

● The Mortgage (95) ● The Assignment (95) ● Title Insurance (95) ● The Owner's Offset Statement (106) ● The Fire Insurance Policy (106) ● Request for Notice (110) ● The First Mortgagee's Statement (110) ● It's Not as Complicated as It Sounds (110) ● You Can Waive Some Requirements (110) ● When the Original Note and Mortgage Are Missing (111) ● Notify the First Mortgagee That You Hold the Second Mortgage (112) ● Who Pays the Transfer Costs? (112) ● An Extra Document (114).

DOUBLE Your Money in SIX YEARS

HOW TO REAP
PROFITS IN
DISCOUNTED
MORTGAGES

1

I TOOK A CHANCE
AND WON

● A SMALL SECOND

Don Gardner, a real estate broker who specializes in mortgages, called me to ask if I might be interested in a small second mortgage. *

I answered with my usual negative phrase, "I'm pretty short of cash."

Gardner laughed. "You always say that."

"It's true," I countered.

"This is only $1,800," he said, "and it's offered at a 40% discount. That's about $1,100—$700 off."

"Pretty risky, huh?"

"I don't think there's as much risk as that discount suggests. The homeowners really want the house. They lived in it for two years under a contract of sale, building up enough for a down payment. Both the husband and wife work; and it's a nice little house in a decent neighborhood."

---

* One property may provide collateral for several loans, with the mortgages ranked as first, second, third, etc.

17

"It still sounds terrible. But I'm listening. Give me the details."

"The present holder of the second mortgage is a man named Forman. The house is stucco—two bedrooms—built on a slab. Fifty-foot lot. It sold for $12,750. The first mortgage is for $10,000, held by Fidelity Savings and Loan. Payments on the first are $75 a month, including 6.6% interest. The second mortgage was originally $1,850 with payments of $18.50, including 7%. The present balance is $1,826.74."

I was writing down these items and figuring at the same time. "The down payment comes out at $900," I put in.

"That's right. The buyers had about $500 built up under the contract-of-sale. They added some extra cash when Forman lined up the $10,000 first mortgage." Gardner paused, and then added some more information, "Forman is a contractor—on a limited scale—and he wants to cash out the deal so he can build another house."

"You mean this is a new house?"

"Less than three years old."

"I'll take a look at it," I said. "What's the address?"

"It's 624 East Farcrest. That's a couple of blocks south of Century Boulevard. You go down the Harbor. . . . ."

"I know the neighborhood," I cut in. "What's the name of the owner?"

"Baker—Martin and Susan."

"You said that both of them work. What do they do?"

"Baker is a heavy-machine operator. His wife is a nurse."

● CHECKING OUT THE OFFER

I drove down and scouted the general neighborhood before looking up the Baker home. I was pleased with the area—a black community with a brand new elementary school and rows of well-kept homes, all recently built, that I estimated to be worth between $12,000 and $18,000. Then I eased along Farcrest Street until I spotted 624.

I was disappointed. The use of a cement slab had placed the house a little lower than the adjoining houses, whose underpinnings were concrete or block foundations that raised them about 3 feet above the Baker house.

I went to the door. Luckily, Mrs. Baker, a black woman about 30 years old, was home. A nurse at a nearby rest home, she worked the afternoon shift. I introduced myself and explained that I was thinking of buying the second mortgage on her house. She was polite, but curt and uncommunicative, for she undoubtedly felt that I was snooping into her financial affairs. However, she did answer a few questions, confirming her occupation and that of her husband.

"As I understand it," I said, "You rented this house from Mr. Forman until you had enough credit for a down payment."

She nodded.

"Do you like the house?" I asked.

She shrugged. "It's a house. I want to live here because there's a good school."

That was the point that tipped the scales. Having seen the excellent school, I decided that Mrs. Baker would go to great lengths to hang on to that house. I went home and called Gardner.

"That Baker house is the poorest one on the block," I told him. "It's worth about $11,000. If I had to foreclose, I'd simply lose the money I put up for the mortgage."

"Are you telling me you don't want this second?"

"I haven't made up my mind. On the one hand, I have a feeling that Mrs. Baker will make the payments. On the other hand, I'm a bit fearful that the property won't give me any security."

"It's a speculation," agreed Gardner. "But you have a lot of very safe paper. You could afford to take one flyer."

"You know I don't like risky seconds."

"Forman is very anxious to raise money. He might even take less."

"How much less?" I asked.

"Why don't you offer him an even thousand?"

"All right," I said, "I'll go for that. Offer him $1,000."

Forman turned down my offer. This was not surprising, since he would net less than $900 after deducting the broker's fee and transfer costs.

● SAVING THE COSTS OF TRANSFER

Gardner, however, did not give up. After asking me to waive a new policy of title insurance, he got an oral confirmation of the current status of the first mortgage. Forman, meanwhile, had agreed to accept my offer on the basis that there would be no transfer costs.

(At this point, I must introduce some terms which may be unfamiliar to you. I will not stop to explain them now, reserving that for later chapters.)

Here's the way we arranged the deal. Since there was no need for a waiting period to prepare the title insurance policy—and

Gardner could get a signed offset statement from the Bakers ahead of time—we could skip the usual escrow procedure.* Forman brought his papers and I brought my checkbook to Gardner's office.

Forman endorsed the note and signed a combined mortgage assignment and request for notice. Gardner put that twofold document into an envelope addressed to the County Recorder with his personal check for the recording fee. Forman handed me the original note and mortgage, now endorsed. I handed Forman a check for $1,000 and Forman gave Gardner a check for his fee. Except for notification of the fire insurance carrier (which Gardner could handle) the transaction was complete.

The Bakers have never been delinquent in their payments on the first mortgage. It is now down to $8,000. They have never been delinquent in their payments on the second mortgage. It is now less than $1,200.

I have received over 12% interest on my investment plus a small portion of each payment as profit on the deal. By the time the Bakers complete their payments, I will receive a total of $827 profit in addition to the steady 12% interest on my investment.

And, for those who might feel that I am getting such high profits at the expense of the homeowners, the Bakers, I would like to point out that my profit comes from Mr. Forman, who discounted the second mortgage. The Bakers are buying a home at a cost of $93.50 per month in an area where rents run about $125.

---

* For those who live in states where escrow procedure is not used, I must explain that this is a method of property transfer handled by an escrow company or department, a bonded institution that takes the place of the lawyer, notary, bank, or Realtor, who holds the money from the buyer and the sale documents from the seller during the transfer period of real estate or mortgages.

2

I SLEEP BETTER
WHEN THE DEAL IS SAFE

● A PROBATE MORTGAGE

Mr. John Banter, an attorney of my acquaintance, mentioned that he was looking for a buyer of a mortgage in a probate case he was handling. It was a first mortgage with an $11,000 balance. The homeowners had paid $4,000 down on a $16,000 house and given the previous owner a $12,000 mortgage. Now, four years later, the balance was down to $11,000, the holder of the mortgage was dead, and the heirs wanted a settlement so they could divide the money.

"As it happens," I told Mr. Banter, "I might be able to dig up something like $10,000. Why don't you give me the name and address of the people who own the house. If it looks all right, I could put in a bid to the estate."

"It's on the east side of town. The address is 2214 Titan. The name of the owner is Rivera."

"I don't know the east side too well," I said. "Where is this Titan Street?"

"I haven't the slightest idea."

"You said it was on the east side."

"The executor told me that. But I haven't gone over there to look at it."

"Never mind. I'll find it. What about the payments?"

"Payments are $80 a month, including 6% interest."

"Are the payments to the estate current?"

"I believe so. But I'd have to check. The Riveras make their payments to a bank and the money is credited directly to the estate bank account."

● APPRAISING THE PROPERTY

Titan was a short street of small, decent stucco houses, a great many Mexican children in the street, flowers in every yard, and some signs of family living in the scars and scratches on doors, windows, and stucco surfaces. I doubted whether the most expensive house on the block would bring $16,000. Maybe, I thought, these houses might run to $14,000, a figure which was still acceptable.

I decided to find out. After stopping my car a half block beyond the Rivera house, I got out and walked along until I saw an elderly Mexican woman working in her yard.

"Buenos dias," I called. "Do you speak English?"

She nodded. "A little."

I quickly manufactured an address, choosing a number between that of the two houses on the other side of the street. "I was trying to find 2248 Titan," I said.

She looked across the street. "There is no 2248. There is only 2244 and 2250."

I pulled out a scrap of paper. "I have 2248. That's what the real estate man said."

"You want to buy a house?"

I nodded.

She studied the houses across the street. "Those houses are not for sale. I know."

"I'll go back to the real estate office to get the right address," I said. "But maybe you can help me—if you live here."

She nodded. "We own this house."

"Have you had it long?"

"Long time."

"How much is it worth?"

"I do not sell it. I live here until I die."

"I don't want to buy your house. I just want to get an idea of how much these houses are worth."

"I not sell. But my friend told me," she pointed to her neighbor's house, "I could sell the house for $18,000."

"Really?"

"Houses are high. Mrs. Hernandez had to pay $18,000."

I followed her glance and guessed that she was referring to a very nice house on high ground a half block away.

Fortified by this rough appraisal, a figure which had raised my own preliminary estimates, I called on the Riveras.

● MY SPANISH WAS LIMITED

Here I ran into a problem. Mrs. Rivera, in halting English, told me that Mr. Rivera did not speak English. Her own English, she explained, was very poor. However, when I tried out a little of my schoolbook Spanish, she helped me. In the process of enjoying my mistakes, her own English seemed to improve. Even so, I was about ready to give up. In a last effort, I told her that a judge would give her mortgage—her payment book—to any person who paid the most money for it.

With considerable excitement, she cried, "These people. They make us pay more?"

I shook my head. "You never have to pay more than $80 a month."

"But the interest. Maybe they make us pay more interest."

"Whoever buys the mortgage has to charge the same interest— 6%."

"What if you buy this mortgage? You will write it down on a paper? You do not take more money?"

I offered to write her a statement on the spot that I would never charge more than $80 a month nor more than 6% interest.

That did it. Her English became almost as good as mine, and all the facts about their employment, savings account, new car, and the history of their upward rise from poverty to home owner-ship were reported to an intent listener—me.

Mr. Rivera appeared, and I sat quietly while Mrs. Rivera told her husband, in Spanish, who I was and what I wanted. When it became apparent, from Mr. Rivera's smiling acceptance of an unknown stranger, that I was getting unreserved approval, I in-terrupted Mrs. Rivera. "Tell him," I said, "that I may not be the person who gets the mortgage. Anyone can put in a bid. Maybe someone else will get it."

Apparently, this had no effect. Mrs. Rivera had made up her mind that I would be the person who would collect that $80 a month.

Their Spanish conversation continued at a rapid pace, finally generating a new idea that caused her to lean forward eagerly.

"You let us pay less, maybe?" she asked. "Seventy dollars a month?"

I shook my head. "You have to pay exactly $80. No more, no less."

● THEY HAD MONEY IN THE BANK

"What if we get some of our money out of the bank? Pay you $1,000—$2,000. Then you take less money?"

I blinked. Her earlier reference to their savings account and their cash purchase of the Chevrolet in the driveway flashed through my mind. I realized that I was talking to thrifty people whose ignorance of English did not prevent them from being financially sound.

I nodded. "You pay $2,000 on the mortgage and I'll reduce the monthly payments."

Knowing that this was a very secure investment, I told the attorney that I would make an offer to purchase the mortgage at a 10% discount. After a week or two, a period which allowed Mr. Banter to solicit other offers, he called to tell me that my offer was satisfactory to him and to the heirs. Mr. Banter then drew up a formal bid for me to sign, I made a down payment, and the sale, in due time, was confirmed by the probate judge.

This has probably been the least profitable of my purchases. But I am receiving 6 2/3% interest, * I am getting monthly profits that will add up to the $1,000 discount by the time the mortgage is paid off, and I have never had a moment's concern about collection of the payments.

---

* At present rates of interest, this may seem low. However, this deal was made at a time when most first mortgages were being made at 6% to 6½%, with an absolute maximum of 6.6%

3

HOW I STARTED

I have presented examples of my investigations and purchases—as an experienced mortgage discounter—which demonstrate the approximate limits of my activity. One was a high-risk, profitable second mortgage; the other was a secure, less profitable first mortgage. Both of them were satisfactory additions to my investment portfolio; both of them contributed to a program that doubled my money in six years.

As a newcomer to this type of investment, it would be well if you kept those limits in mind as you travel the road I have traveled. But you have to get on the road first. You have to get started. Before we start you off, however, let us go back a dozen years and see how I started.

My wife and I had just paid the last mortgage payment on the home in which we had lived for 20 years. The house was getting old, two of our children were gone, and we were having our first thoughts about plans for our senior years. My wife and I talked about the house, which needed a new roof, a remodeled kitchen, and a great many other improvements. Then we reached a decision which we considered very brilliant. We would sell the house, as is, to some young couple for a low down payment and a long period of monthly payments. The down payment would give us enough money to buy new furniture, and the monthly payments would subsidize our rent in a modern, up-to-date apartment.

Everything went according to plan. In a few months, we were in a beautiful apartment with our new furniture. The monthly payments of $85, paid by a young man who was busy remodeling our old house, provided a substantial part of our monthly rent.

A year later, everything changed. The escrow department of our bank notified us that the young man had resold our house, the deal was being financed by a savings and loan company, and we were to receive the remaining balance of the mortgage debt on that house.

● WHAT WOULD I DO WITH $12,500?

The news that we were to receive $12,500 in cash seemed, to me, to be a minor disaster. "What am I going to do with $12,500?" I asked my wife.

"Put it in a savings account or buy government bonds," she replied.

"But we were getting 6% before," I pointed out. "If we put it in bonds, we'll be lucky to get 4%."

"I don't know why anyone should complain about receiving thousands of dollars," said my wife. "I remember the days when you thought $100 was a fortune."

"I was counting on that 6% interest to help us pay our rent."

"Look," said my wife, "we had a mortgage on the house. Now it's being paid off. But there must be other mortgages. If you could find another mortgage, we could start getting monthly payments again. And we would probably get 6% interest, too."

"Where do you go to find mortgages?" I asked.

"In the newspaper," said my wife. "When I was looking in the want ads for apartments, I'm sure I saw something about mortgages."

I got the paper and hunted through the want ads until I found the column headed, "Mortgages for Sale." Among the listings was an item offering a $12,400 first mortgage with monthly payments of $125 at a 5.5% interest rate. It was priced at $11,900.

This truly remarkable coincidence—a mortgage that almost duplicated the one which was being prepaid—could not be ignored.

I showed the item to my wife. "It doesn't pay as much interest as we were getting," I said. "But it does pay more than 4%. And we can make $500 extra." (Neither my wife nor I knew that the difference between the mortgage balance and the mortgage buyer's cost is known as a discount.)

We went to the office of the broker, a young man named Gardner, and I told him we were interested in the advertised first mortgage.

"That's a very good one," he said.

"I want to be sure it's safe," I told him.

"You couldn't find a better one. The house sold for $23,000 with a $6,000 down payment. The original note was for $17,000, so you can see that payments have been made for many years. The owner is an engineer who gets a good salary."

"I'd like to look at the house," I said.

"Naturally," said Gardner, "No one buys a note without checking the security."

● INNOCENTS ABROAD

He gave me the name and address of the owner; and my wife and I—like two babes in the woods—went out to look at a house on a corner lot that was much nicer and somewhat larger than the house we had sold the year before.

This was the way we appraised it. We looked at it from the front and from the side. (It never occurred to us to knock at the door and talk to the owners.) Then we walked up the street and looked at the other houses in that block. "Do you think these houses are worth $23,000?" I asked my wife.

"They must be worth $20,000," she replied. "And this is a corner house, with a big lot, so it might sell for $23,000." (The actual market price in that area had already risen to a figure above $27,000.)

"The important thing to ask is what we would do if they stopped making the payments. We might have to foreclose. And then we might have to live in it."

"That would be all right," said my wife. "It's a lot better than our old house."

"It's a long way from my job," I said.

"It's not that far," declared my wife. "If we could get a $23,000 house for $11,900, you ought to be willing to drive a few extra miles."

"I guess it would be all right to buy the mortgage," I said. So we drove back to Gardner's office to tell him we would take it.

But we were not through with our first day's adventure in the world of real estate financing. As we made plans to arrange for completing the transaction, I told Mr. Gardner about the source of our money—our own house, which we had converted into a mortgage that had been paying us 6% interest. In response, Gardner gave us our first lesson in mortgage discounting. This first mortgage we were buying had a low discount because it was extra safe. Nevertheless, that $500 discount did increase our return from 5½% to almost 6%. For higher interest rates and better profits, he explained, one had to buy second mortgages.

● SECOND MORTGAGES HAVE BIGGER DISCOUNTS

I asked about second mortgages and was told that the combination of a higher rate and a bigger discount generally produced a return of 10% or more. Also, one did not need so much capital because there were many second mortgages with due balances of $2,000 to $3,000.

"Do you have any like that now?" I asked.

"Yes, we have several; some with discounts as high as 20%," replied Gardner.

I hurried to qualify my question. "They would have to be safe."

"I understand that," said the broker. He then asked how much capital I might wish to invest, over and above the first mortgage we had already arranged to purchase.

"We have about $4,000 in government bonds," I explained. "Perhaps we could sell half of them. That would give us $2,000 to put into a second mortgage."

Gardner went through his files and selected a folder. Then he gave us the details of a second mortgage that might be suitable for us. Originally $3,000, it had been paid down to $2,400. The payments were $30 a month, including 6% interest. There was a first mortgage of less than $7,000, which had been reduced from $8,500. The homeowner and his wife both worked—the husband as an auto mechanic, the wife as a teacher. And there was a 10% discount, which meant that we could buy it for $2,160.

"But the interest rate is only 6%," I pointed out. "You said that second mortgages paid about 10%."

"It's very difficult to figure the true interest on a discounted mortgage," said Gardner. "This one has a maturity date that is only two years away. If it is paid off ahead of time, your interest and profit could produce a rate of 20%. If it paid off at maturity, it would come out at something like 15%. If you gave an extension of a year or two, your interest return would drop to a 10% figure."*

---

* You should begin to use the Yield Tables at the back of the book (page 199). The tables do not present the yields for a two-year due date, but we can use the three-year section in the 6% table (page 201) to check the accuracy of Gardner's last figure. Use the first line in the table—10% Discount—and look across to the 1.25 payback rate (the $30 monthly payment divided by the $2,400 balance). The correct yield is 10½%.

"I'm not sure I understand all this," I said.

"I'll tell you what I'll do," Gardner declared. "I'll give you the address and you go look at the property. If you like the deal, you can have the paper for $2,100. That's a $300 profit."

As my wife was already late for another appointment, I went out to look at this offer alone. The property proved to be a stucco house very much like the house we had sold, though I did not think the district was quite as good as our former neighborhood. Since I was a little nervous about this possible investment, I decided I wanted to talk to the owners. But no one answered my knock. So I walked down the street to take a look at the other houses in that block. I saw a man in his front yard who looked like he might be the owner. I stopped and asked him what these houses were worth.

He shrugged his shoulders. "I couldn't say," he replied. "But I figure my place is worth $20,000."

"Twenty thousand!" I exclaimed.

"I've got a rental in the back," he said, "over the garage."

"Oh."

● THE ECONOMY CAR TIPPED THE SCALES

Without any further attempt at appraisal, I returned to my car and sat there looking at the house with the $7,000 first mortgage and the $2,400 second, wondering if there was enough value to protect a very scared potential buyer of that second mortgage. Just then a Volkswagen came up the street and turned into the driveway of the house. A woman got out and carried her groceries into the house.

"Hmmm," I said to myself. "That must be the teacher. I guess they are watching their nickels and dimes. People who drive economy cars ought to make their home payments."

I went home and called Gardner to tell him we would take that second mortgage.

● HOW THOSE INVESTMENTS TURNED OUT

The 5.5% first mortgage was not the kind of high-profit investment that allows one to double his money in a short time, but it has proved to be an excellent security for me. It has served as collateral for several bank loans, it produces a dependable $125 in cash every month, and it gives me a feeling of serene confidence whenever I consider that first ultraconservative investment.

The second mortgage was something of an emotional yo-yo. Those homeowners may have been economical with their second car, but they proved to be perpetually late with their payments. Every month I went through a painful process of extracting that

$30 installment. A year went by, and I had become so engrossed in making those collections that I forgot all about the approaching due date.

Then, many months before the maturity date, I received a letter from a savings and loan company. My slow-paying homeowners had arranged for a new and larger first mortgage that would pick up my second. I was instructed to forward my note and mortgage to them. In a few days, they told me, I would be paid the entire balance still due.

When I received the final payment on that second mortgage, I sat down to figure how much I had made. In 15 months, from an investment of $2,100, I had received a total return of $2,570. As near as I could figure, this meant that the true annual interest was about 18%. I promptly forgot all about my grievous months of collecting payments; I was ready to buy another second mortgage.

4

MY PROFIT COMES
FROM THE DISCOUNT

● YOU MAY THINK IT'S MAGIC

At the end of the preceding chapter, there was an account of something that looked like magic—the magic that changed a 6% investment into an 18% return. A great many readers, familiar with discounts, may have a thorough understanding of how they produce extra profits for an investor. If you are in that group, you can skip this chapter and go ahead to the next, where I present my advice for your first steps in mortgage investments. On the other hand, if you are not sure you understand the nature of discount operations, you should read this short chapter, in which I will explain discounting as carefully and clearly as possible.

Most people are accustomed to: (1) earnings from a specified rate of interest and/or (2) profits from the rise in the market price of a purchased security. Conditioned to this investment outlook, it is not easy to see how extra money can be made when the rate of interest is fixed (such as a 7% rate on a mortgage) and the debt to be repaid (the principal amount of a mortgage) is also fixed. The secret, which you must completely understand, lies in the discount.

● GET A PAPER AND PENCIL

Instead of reading the balance of this chapter in relaxed comfort, I suggest that you put down the book and go get a paper and pencil. We are going to work some problems—and you should actually do the problems yourself.

● PERHAPS YOU KNOW SOMETHING ABOUT BONDS

Let us begin by using an example with which you may be more familiar. If you will look in the financial section of your daily newspaper, you will find—in several places—listings of bond prices. In one place will be the list of government bonds. In another you will find a list of bonds traded on the New York Bond Market, which includes railroad bonds, utility bonds, industrial bonds, foreign bonds, and bonds traded on the American Exchange. Although these bonds are always in $1,000 certificates, the prices are quoted on a $100 basis. Thus, a United Gas Pipeline bond, listed as bearing a 5.75% rate and due in 1980, is quoted at 71 to 80 for a $1,000 certificate that can be bought or sold at $710 to $800. A treasury bond, listed as bearing a 4% rate and due in 1980, is quoted at 74 to 75 for a $1,000 certificate that can be bought or sold at $740 to $750.

Let us figure out the actual interest you would earn if you bought either of the previous bonds. Suppose you bought the United Gas Pipeline bond for $720. You would receive a 5.75% rate on a $1,000 certificate—$57.50 a year, paid to you in two semiannual installments of $28.75 each. But your investment was only $720, so you are receiving a current interest income ($57.50 on $720) that calculates to be 7.99%. On the treasury bond, purchased at $750, you would receive $40 a year, which produces a current interest rate of exactly 5 1/3%.

This is what you should have on your paper:

	.0798+			.053+
$720	$57.50		$750	$40.00
	50 40			37.50
	7 100			2 500
	6 480			2 250
	6200			250
	5760			
	440			

Looking at those figures and comparing them with reported returns of 7 to 9% on bonds, you could well ask whether I have chosen very conservative examples of bond investments. Not at all. I have chosen typical examples of bond investments which actually earn an interest *yield* of 7.5% to 9%. The United Gas Pipeline bond will show a 9%* return; the treasury bond will show a 7.6% return. This higher return comes from the discount, which is the difference between what you paid for the bond and what you will receive at maturity.

When you bought the United Gas Pipeline bond at $720 you acquired a $280 built-in profit, because you will receive $1,000 in 1980. And you must spread that $280 profit over the ten-year period and add a portion of it each year to the $57.50 annual interest to arrive at the true interest return. After making an adjustment for the fact that the discount payback is a deferred payment, you arrive at a figure of 9%*. This true interest on a bond is known as the yield. In the case of the treasury bond, the addition of the $250 profit to your earnings (when the bond matures in 1980) is already calculated right there in the financial listing in the newspaper. It is given as a yield of 7.64%. You don't have to do any complicated arithmetic problem because you are told, in the quotation, that your apparent 5 1/3% interest rate is actually a true return of 7.64%.

● THE PROFITS KEEP GROWING

If you have mastered this example of bond interest calculation, we are ready to talk about the same thing in the business of buying another kind of security—a mortgage. Again, the secret of the higher income is in the discount. It is possible to buy a mortgage with a low fixed interest rate, such as 7%, and a fixed amount of

---

* My stock broker's bond book gives the figure as a small fraction below 9%. My own calculation, after allowing $160 to reduce the $280 discount profit to present value, comes out at 9.6%.
Here is my arithmetic:

Discount profit $280.00
Allowance to reduce deferred profit to present value 160.00
Profit on current basis $120.00
Annual profit $12.00
Annual interest 57.50
Total annual yield $69.50

$$
\begin{array}{r}
.096+ \\
\$720 \overline{\smash{\big)}\ \$69.50} \\
64\ 80 \\
\overline{4\ 700} \\
4\ 320 \\
\overline{380}
\end{array}
$$

debt, such as $4,000, that will produce a truly fantastic rate of return. (The example I am giving is not taken out of my hat. It is an actual offer that appeared on a current broker's list that I have before me.)

The mortgage is a second. The balance is approximately $4,000. The rate of interest is 7%. The monthly payment is $50. It is offered at a 25% discount. Its maturity date is two and one-half years hence. It is, according to the stated information, a reasonably safe security on a good home in a suburb which has a considerable Mexican-American population.

Let us figure the actual returns you would receive if you bought this second mortgage and required the homeowner to make that balloon payment at the end of two and one-half years. Throughout the period of payments you would receive 7% interest calculated on the amount owed, which would start at $4,000 and drop slightly each month. But you would figure the current interest on your investment on the basis of a cost that would start at $3,000 and drop by exactly the same ratio as the mortgage balance dropped. Your current rate of interest, therefore, would be 9 1/3%.

Here are the figures:
Balance due $4,000.00
Interest rate   07
Interest (per year) $280.00

$$\begin{array}{r} .093+ \\ \$3,000\overline{)\$280.00} \\ 270\ 00 \\ \hline 10\ 000 \\ 9\ 000 \\ \hline 1\ 000 \end{array}$$

Your investment

As pointed out earlier, however, this is not the full yield. To obtain that rate, you must spread the $1,000 profit over a two-and-one-half-year period and add it to your interest income. Your yield will figure to be almost 22%.* (It might appear to be higher if you did not allow for the present value of the $1,000 discount payback you receive—a small portion with each monthly installment; the bulk of it in two and one-half years.)

That difference between the 9 1/3% current interest rate and the true yield of 22% is the big profit made by the mortgage investor who buys mortgages at a discount. The amount of that profit is determined by a combination of the same factors that produce the

---

* If you will refer to the 7% Yield Table at the back of the book, you will find that the yield for three years is 19½%. For the shorter period of two and one-half years, the yield (not tabulated) is higher.

higher yield for bond investors, with one added factor. The similar factors are: (1) the amount of the discount (the difference between the cost price and the face of the obligation), with the greater discount producing the greater profit, and (2) the length of time between the time of purchase and the maturity date, with the shorter time producing the greater profit. The added factor that the mortgage investor has to consider is the amount of the monthly installment, with the larger installment producing the greater profit.

As with any investment, the mortgage investor must first judge the safety of the security he buys. He must then be able to work out the arithmetic of interest rates on the amount he invests, with the all-important discount payback properly considered. His final step is to balance the yield against the safety, trying for the highest possible return while not unduly risking his capital.

● YOU CAN BARGAIN

I was sitting in a mortgage broker's office one day while he talked to a customer on the telephone. It was evident, from the first phrases, that the man on the other end of the line had just returned from an investigation of a house that secured a second mortgage in a lower-priced home area.

Here is the broker's end of the conversation:

"Twenty-five per cent is the best discount you can get."
. . . .
"I know that. But the homeowner has a steady job and his pay record is good. It's an excellent deal at 25%."
. . . .
"No. I've already suggested 30%. He isn't interested. He said he'd rather keep the paper."
. . . .
"All right. I'll be here until 5 o'clock."

You can fill in the blanks of that conversation quite easily. The potential buyer, after asking if the seller might accept a larger discount, had made some statement about the poor quality of the investment. He had then offered a 30% discount, which he wanted the broker to pass on to the seller. In the end, he had declared that he wanted to think it over.

This truthful report is given to suggest the amount of bargaining that goes on as a mortgage discounter attempts to increase his *yield* by getting a bigger discount. The bargainer in this case would probably not succeed. In other cases, as in the first example in this book (the Baker deal), a larger discount can be obtained.

● PRICES OF HOUSES ARE NEGOTIABLE

In buying a home, you generally expect to bargain. When a house is offered at $30,000, you offer $27,000. Perhaps the seller drops his price by $500. If you hold out, perhaps the seller will come down to your price—or you might compromise at $28,500. The final outcome depends on several factors: the anxiety of the homeowner to sell, your desire to buy, and the condition of the housing market.

Bargaining for mortgages is not quite so general. The seller of a mortgage, who is usually a person of some substance, is not going to give it away (unless there's something wrong with it), because he can usually take it off the market and settle for a slower cash-out of his investment from the monthly payments. The buyer cannot make his offer too low; some other investor will step in and pick it up. Nevertheless, the amount of the discount, determined by experienced brokers and sophisticated buyers and sellers on the basis of the quality of the mortgage and the state of the money market, is a matter for bargaining on a limited scale.

The point to remember is that the discount is the factor that converts ordinary interest into a profitable yield. And that yield is determined at the time you make the purchase of the mortgage. Before you sign your name to the mortgage purchase agreement, you might suggest a bigger discount. It doesn't hurt to try, and you might pick up another $100 in profit.

5

YOUR STARTING GUIDE

● READ THE WANT ADS

Now that you know how I got started and, hopefully, understand exactly how the discount factor increases your mortgage investment income, it is time for you to get into this business. Your first move is to read the ads in your daily newspaper under the heading, "Mortgages for Sale." Then you call the brokers who put in the advertisements; get all the information on the particular mortgages advertised; drive out to see the properties that secure the offered mortgages; and stop and talk to the first homeowner on your list, checking the information you have been given about original sales price, mortgage totals, monthly payments, taxes, etc. Ask about the homeowner's employment, his children, his background, etc. If you can open up your interview with general conversation, you will have an opportunity to glean items that may tell you something about the homeowner's character and credit.

If the homeowners are not home, go to the house next door. Don't damage the homeowner's credit by mentioning mortgage debt and don't suggest that you are a long-lost rich relative from Indiana. The simple statement that you wished to talk to Mr. So-and-So about a business matter not connected with collection of debts may be sufficient to start a flood of more extensive information than you would receive if you talked to the homeowner himself; or you could pretend to be an appraiser from a realty firm making a survey of the entire district—which might give you a better opening to discuss all property values in that area.

During your survey trip, either before or after your checkup on the specific property, you should drive around the neighborhood. If you see a man fixing a fence or mowing a lawn, stop and talk to him about property values.

You then repeat this procedure with the other offerings on your list. (Since this is a trial run, it is not absolutely necessary to interview each homeowner.)

At the conclusion of your evaluation excursion, call each broker and give him an excuse for not being in the market for the particular deal he offered you. But don't hang up until he has your name, address, and telephone number. You want to be on his list for information on future offerings, which he will usually send out in the form of typed or printed lists.

You have learned something about judging people and property values. You have also had a chance to appraise the quality and type of mortgage that the various brokers handle. Some brokers tend to specialize in very conservative mortgages with relatively low discounts, while others deal in high-risk, high-discount paper. Having made a mental note of these differences between the brokers, you are now ready to think of making your first purchase.

● A BROKER'S LIST OF OFFERINGS

In a week or two, perhaps, you receive a broker's list such as the one I am presenting—an actual page of offerings (except #481 and #484) reproduced just as it came to me:

(In the State of California, almost all real estate obligations—commonly called mortgages—are in the legal form of deeds of trust or trust deeds, which are abbreviated to T.D.)

For Sale

Loan 478. $10,960 first T.D. At 5% discount, you pay $10,412. The note pays $96.50 or more per mo. incl. 9½%, all due 10 yrs. Secured by two 2 BR homes on a 50'x125' level lot at 22155 Delvalle, Woodland Hills, Calif. that recently sold for $15,000 with $4,000 cash down payment, plus owner has spent considerable time and money remodeling and redecorating.

Loan 479. $3,781 second T.D. At 40% discount, you pay $2,262.50. The note pays $30 or more incl. 8½% until paid. Secured by 1035 East Lancaster Blvd., Lancaster, Calif. that sold on 10-24-69 for $19,000 with $1,900 cash down payment and a new $13,300 S&L first T.D. Lot is 87'x127.5.'

Loan 480. $2,250 second T.D. At 30% discount, you pay $1,475. The note pays $24 or more per mo. incl. 7ᵊ until paid. It has an acceleration clause. Secured by a 3 BR stucco home at 8158 Virginia Ave., South Gate that sold on 4-4-69 for $16,500 and a new $12,000 S&L first T.D. $1,600 down.

Loan 481. $2,600 second T.D. At 30% discount, you pay $1,820. The note pays $30 per mo. incl. 7½%, all due two years. Secured by 2 BR stucco home on corner lot at 1478 West 106th St. that sold on 5-15-67 for $18,000 with $2,000 cash down payment and $13,000 S&L first T.D. Lot is 60'x110.'

Loan 482. $3,597 second T.D. At 35% discount, you pay $2,335. The note pays $38.14 or more per mo. incl. 7½% until paid. It has an acceleration clause. Secured by a 3 BR stucco home at 15536 South Harris Ave., Compton that sold on 4-21-69 for $33,500 with $3,400 cash down. There are also two 2 BR apartments plus a 3-car garage and a single carport. Lot is 66'x166.'

Loan 483. $10,500 first T.D. At 20% discount on probate bid sale, you pay $8,400. The note pays $100 or more per mo. incl. 7%, all due March 1973. Secured by two old units at 2354 South Hillcrest near Crenshaw and Adams that sold in April 1969 for $12,000 with $1,000 cash down. The owner has since converted it into a single home for his own residence.

Loan 484. $2,702 second T.D. At appr. 26% discount, you pay $2,000. The note pays $30 per mo. incl. 7.2%, all due 9-10-76. Secured by 3 BR stucco home at 9342 Westbourne Ave., Huntington Park, that sold on 8-10-69 for $24,500 with $3,000 cash down and $18,500 S&L first T.D. Owner has made extra payments on second T.D. Lot is 64'x124.'

Loan 485. $4,110 second T.D. At 25% discount, you pay $3,080. The note pays $42 or more per mo., all due 11-3-72 incl. 7½%. Secured by 2 BR custom, 10-year-old stucco home on two lots at 8834 Wonderland Ave., L.A. Hollywood Hills that sold on 12-3-69 for $32,500 with $4,000 cash down.

Loan 486. $10,353 first T.D. At 9% discount, you pay $9,400. The note pays $200 or more per mo. incl. 6%; will pay out in 4 yrs., 11 mos. Seasoned 6 yrs. Secured by a stucco duplex at <u>13553 East Tedemory Drive, Whittier, Calif.</u> Taxes are $423 per yr. Lot is approx. 62'x102.'

Loan 487. $50,000 first T.D. At 30% discount, you pay $35,000. The note pays $1,250 quarterly incl. 7%, all due 2-2-80. It has release clauses and acceleration clause. Secured by 40 acres less highway which is <u>Encinal Canyon Road, Malibu</u> that goes through the property. It sold on 3-10-70 for $65,000 with $15,000 cash down. Taxes are $3,094. Legal is SW¼, NE¼, of Section 22, Township 2 North, Range 20 West.

You cross off Loan #478 because you do not have $10,000. You go right past #479 because Lancaster is too far away. You consider #480 for quite a while but finally eliminate it, for the moment, because you would prefer a mortgage with a due date. In the end, you decide to investigate #481 and #484. You call the broker, confirm that these two offers are still available, and get all the additional information obtainable.

● SOME PEOPLE WON'T TALK

You drive down to 106th Street and find a small, decent-looking corner house that looks as if it should be worth $18,000. So you walk up and ring the bell. After a long interval, you hear a woman's voice asking what you want. You discover that the hidden voice is coming from a barely open window on your left. You turn to speak to the window, explaining that you are interested in buying their second mortgage, which has been offered for sale.

"I don't talk to strangers," says the voice.

"I only wanted to confirm the information I received from the broker," you tell her.

"I told you I don't talk to strangers."

"But you did buy this house three years ago," you persist.

"This is our house, Mister."

"I know that. Perhaps I could talk to your husband if you would tell me where to find him. Is he at work?"

"My husband don't talk to strangers about our business, either."

You give up on this one and leave—you drop it right off your list. Later, you will tell the broker that you didn't get enough information from the homeowner, and you won't accept the broker's report of what the facts are. He may be the most honest man in the city, but the information he will give you will be hearsay, which is not very good in court or in business. You can cross off this proposition without prejudice or disappointment because there will be plenty of homeowners who will be cooperative about information. (Sometimes they talk so much you can hardly get away from them.)

● TRY, TRY AGAIN

You get in your car and start for Huntington Park to check up on Loan #484. On the way, you run over the details of this offer: it is a seven-year $2,702 second mortgage with $30 monthly payments, including 7.2% interest, which can be purchased for an even $2,000. The original amount was $3,000, but the homeowners, who have had the house for a year, have made some extra payments to reduce the balance. The sales price of the house was $24,500 on which they had made a $3,000 down payment. The first mortgage (according to the broker) was originally $18,500. With payments of $128 a month, it should now be paid down to a balance of about $18,000.

When you get to the place on Westbourne Avenue, you find a young man who is exactly the opposite of the close-mouthed woman you have just left. You talk to him in his backyard, where he is busy putting up a swing set for his two small boys. He has a good job with 12 years seniority. He knows the former owners, a couple whose marriage had ended in divorce, and he is eager to tell you all about their troubles.

"That wife took the poor guy for everything—this house, the furniture, alimony, and child support."

"If she got all that," you respond, "why does she want to sell the second mortgage? Why doesn't she just sit tight and take your $30 payments until the balance comes due?"

"She wants to go to Cleveland," he explains. "I've heard she's got an old boy friend back there."

You like this deal, but you don't commit yourself until you do a little figuring. You always have to consider the possibility of trouble. Maybe the homeowner who had just expressed his sympathy for a fellow-husband may find himself in the same situation. If, out of a domestic battle, you are forced to take over this property, do you have the reserves to carry the house?

You can estimate that the foreclosure costs will be $250, and over a four-month period, the payments on the first mortgage will be $512. But (assuming you have $2,800 in cash) you would have $800 left after putting up the asking price of $2,000. You decide to go ahead and buy this second mortgage. (If you live in a state where the redemption period is longer than three or four months, you must allow a cash reserve large enough to cover first mortgage payments through the period of the legal redemption period. So far as I know, the longest redemption period permitted anywhere is one year.)

Now you wait, with some nervousness, until the wonderful day when that first $30 arrives in the mail. You have earned your first $16.21 in interest and $3.59 in discount pay-back profit.

● YOU ARE ON YOUR WAY

You are now in a position to consider another mortgage purchase. Perhaps, if you had more than the assumed $2,800, you already have enough cash for a second purchase. On the other hand, you may have to wait until you have saved another $1,000. In either case, you can go into the second deal on the basis of a different approach to the calculation of a cash reserve. You don't have to keep backing for both mortgages, because your original reserve will serve to protect you on both if the costs of carrying the first mortgages are the same. It is extremely unlikely that two of your carefully selected investments will run into trouble at the same time.

To put this into figures, let's assume that you started with $5,200 in cash. After you pay $2,000 for the original mortgage and allow $800 for your reserve, you still have $2,400 to invest in a similar deal. The $800, kept in a bank account, serves to back up both of your investments.

The same reasoning applies to a third and fourth investment of the same size, with a similar potential obligation in their first mortgages. Since it is unlikely that all of the debtor homeowners will default at the same time, you can use reserve funds which you maintain to cover the costs of foreclosure on one mortgage as a reserve for several mortgages. Naturally, as your investments multiply, it would be well to increase your reserve until such time as your monthly cash receipts provide a continuous reserve. (Although I have specified cash, you will understand that such a reserve can also be maintained with securities, eligibility for a bank loan, the substantial capital position of a relative or associate who would be in a position to assist you, or, as mentioned above, a substantial cash flow.)

● USE OTHER PEOPLE'S MONEY

As time goes by, your own net worth, including the mortgages you own, may become strong enough to warrant the use of bank credit. In the early stages, you may be able to borrow money because you earn a good salary, especially if you can demonstrate (by steady additions to your bank savings) that your regular income is more than your living expenses. Later on, you may use one of your mortgages as collateral for a bank loan. This is very convenient when a favorable mortgage offer comes up that is priced at a figure a little higher than your ready cash.

Let's suppose that you are offered a seasoned $4,900 first mortgage at $4,400 at a time when you only have $3,000. Borrow $2,500 from your bank. This will pay for the mortgage and allow you to keep $1,100 as your reserve.

You may find, if you are dealing with a branch bank, that the man who handles your application is not an expert on mortgages or mortgage discounting. He knows what a mortgage loan is, but he may not be familiar with all the factors in this business because he engages in such things as salary loans, automobile financing, business inventory loans, and home improvement loans. You must be prepared to explain your investments and your activities in the mortgage business—including the fact that your income will consist of interest *and discount pay-back profits.* At the time of my first bank loan, when interest rates were much lower, the banker was disturbed because my 5½% mortgage collateral was less than the 6% I was expected to pay. I had to explain that I was going to use the money to buy a mortgage with an actual current rate of almost 9% and a yield of over 12%.

● SELL YOUR OWN HOUSE AND MOVE INTO AN APARTMENT

If you intend to engage in the mortgage discounting business up to the limit of your resources, and to take some risks to get the biggest discounts, you may consider this final suggestion: *If you own your own house—sell it.*

There are two reasons for this seemingly drastic advice. In the first place, it will give you added capital to pursue your mortgage discounting business. In the second place, it will give you an opportunity to invest in high-risk, high-discount second mortgages. You need to choose only those which you would be willing to take over personally.

I know a man who started his mortgage discounting while living in a rented house. His original second mortgage purchase was on a duplex a few blocks from his own residence. He was prepared, if the owner defaulted, to foreclose on the property, move into half the duplex, and let the rental payments of the other half carry the first mortgage until he could sell the duplex. The owner, however, did not allow the payments to default; the owner's equity soon reached such a substantial figure that my friend knew a problem would be highly unlikely. He then bought a high-discount second mortgage on another house that he and his wife would be ready and willing to occupy.

He is still renting, but he is receiving enough interest income to pay his rent. In addition, he is earning a substantial profit on the discounted portion of the principal pay-back on his mortgages.

● HOW TO FIGURE YOUR DISCOUNT PROFIT

Although we shall be discussing this more fully in the chapter on bookkeeping, it would not be amiss to stop here and break down that first $30 installment payment, given in the example earlier in this chapter, so you can see how it works out to a specific discount pay-back profit. First we go back to the $2,702 mortgage which you bought for $2,000. If you divide the $2,702 into the $702 discount, you arrive at a figure of 26%. (You already knew this, of course, because the discount percentage was given in the broker's list.) Now, let us figure that first $30 payment. At a 7.2% rate, the interest portion of the $30 is $16.21. Subtracting the $16.21 from the $30 results in a balance of $13.79, which is applied against the $2,702 debt. This $13.79 is the principal payment. But you bought that mortgage principal at a 26% discount. So you can apply the 26% rate to the $13.79 and arrive at a profit figure of $3.59.

```
Installment payment ...................................$30.00
Monthly interest (on $2,702) ...........................16.21
Credited to principal ..................................$13.79
Discount percentage .....................................  .26
                                                        ─────
                                                        8274
                                                        2758
                                                       ─────
Discount pay-back profit.............................. $3.5854
```

Every month you can multiply the principal portion of the installment payment by 26% to calculate your discount profit. Six years later, at the due date, there will be a remaining balance of about $1,460, which comes due as a final balloon payment. Your profit on that would be $379.60.

A Percentage Problem

> If you are serious about investing in mortgages at a discount, you might like to try your hand at calculating the current interest rate and the approximate yield. For the current rate, you calculate one year's interest on the basis of the first month's payment (7.2% of $2,702) and divide it by $2,000. This is the true current interest rate.
>
> For the approximate yield, you multiply the regular monthly $30 payment by 72. Add the $1,460 final balance to this total. This is your total of receipts for six years. Subtract the $2,000 cost to find your six-year profit. Now subtract $200, which is an estimated allowance to adjust deferred discount pay-back profits to present value. Divide this by 6 to obtain your approximate annual yield total. Divide this by $1,580, your average adjusted-cost basis, and you have your estimated percentage of yield.

Your current annual interest rate should have been 9.7%. Your yield should have been 14.98%. If you got both problems right, you are a statistician and will make more money in this business than I have. If you got the current rate but missed on the yield, you are in good company. A majority of mortgage discounters know their true current interest rates but they aren't sure about their exact yields. They only know they are making a lot of money.

For those who had trouble with the second part of the problem there is hope. You can use a Yield Table.

Look in the 7.2% Yield Table on page 204 at the back of this book. In the "Due in 6 years" section, at the 25% discount line, you will find your yield to be 14½% on a 1% pay-back rate and 15½% on a 1.25% pay-back rate. Since a $30 payment on a $2,702 balance is a 1.11% pay-back rate, you can estimate your yield to be almost halfway between 14½% and 15½%—or a fraction below 15%.

6

I WAS SURPRISED TO DISCOVER
I WAS BUYING NOTES

● THE PROMISSORY NOTE

Let us stop here to talk about the securities in which we are investing. The common term with which you are familiar is mortgage. In California and several other states, however, the actual mortgage instrument is a trust deed. But the important papers that we actually buy are neither mortgages nor trust deeds. *They are promissory notes,* which are accompanied by mortgages or trust deeds that pledge specific parcels of real estate as guarantees that the notes will be paid. If you will go back to the preceding chapter and go over the broker's list again, you will see that every listing refers to both the mortgage (trust deed) and the note.

We will defer the precise description and explanation of the nature of the actual documents because our first concern is to find out about the market—the buying and selling of these investments—and understand what they represent, how

46

they originate, and how they become available. The best way to do this is to outline a fictitious home-purchase transaction.

● A GOOD DOWN PAYMENT

John and Mary Ward decided to buy a house from Fred Grant. The agreed price was $26,000, but the Wards had only $5,000 in cash. This, of course, is a normal situation in our society. The Wards could use the $5,000 as a down payment and complete the purchase of the house with installment payments. To arrange the transaction, the Wards and Mr. Grant went to an escrow company (or attorney) and filled out escrow instructions or a sales agreement.

The Wards signed a promissory note for $21,000 in which they agreed to pay Mr. Grant $150 a month, including 7% interest, until the debt was paid. They also signed a mortgage, which had a great deal of fine print, that required the Wards to keep the house in repair and pay the taxes. The fine print also stated what would happen if the Wards violated deed restrictions or did not make the payments on the note. In the next few days, Mr. Grant delivered his title papers to the escrow company and the Wards paid in their $5,000 down payment. Then they waited while the escrow company arranged for a title insurance policy,* obtained an endorsement of Mr. Grant's fire insurance policy, calculated the pro rata of taxes and insurance premiums, and prepared the transfer deed.

While this deal is pending, let's stop and call attention to an important point. The Wards signed *two* papers to cover that $21,000 indebtedness. The first one, the note, was like any other promissory note, except that it specified installment payments and provided for reduction of the principal. The second paper, the mortgage, was a lien on the property (or, in trust deed states, it was an inactive transfer of title to a neutral party). In any case, it pledged their new house as security for the $21,000 debt.

At the end of the transfer period the Wards got their deed, which had been recorded; the title insurance policy; a copy of the fire insurance policy on the house, now listing them as owners; a payment book; and the keys to the house. Mr. Grant got $5,000; the note; the mortgage, which had been recorded; a copy of the title insurance policy; a copy of the fire insurance policy naming him as mortgagee; and a payment book.

---

* In some states this might be an abstract of title, certificate of title, or commitment of title.

● THE MORTGAGE WAS OFFERED FOR SALE

For a time, Mr. Grant was satisfied to collect his $150 each month. Later, when the balance had dropped to $20,000, he decided he wanted to go back to a little farm in Arkansas. He notified a broker that he wanted to sell his mortgage. He wanted the full $20,000 still due, but the broker would not handle it on that basis. Mr. Grant had to agree to discount it, and the discount could have been 5, 10, or 15%.

This is an example of a transaction that produced what is known as a purchase-money mortgage that comes on the market. You will notice that this was a case where the seller owned the property without any indebtedness and there was no savings and loan company involved. You will probably say that you never heard of such a transaction; that no one owns property without some debt; and that there are always savings and loan firms that finance the sales, take the mortgages, and file them away in their vaults. Thus, first mortgages of this type would not appear on the market for a private party to buy at discounted prices. But I can assure you that such mortgages do come on the market. According to one real estate authority, the number of first mortgages in private hands runs to an estimated 15 or 20% of the total.

Without debating that point further, let us go on to examine a transaction which occurs more frequently—where there is an unpaid mortgage debt owed to a savings and loan company and the buyers are a little short on the required down payment. To keep their roles clear, we'll use the same names.

● THEY DIDN'T HAVE THE DOWN PAYMENT

John and Mary Ward were buying a house from Fred Grant on which he still owed $10,000. The agreed price was $26,000, but the Wards only had $2,000 for the down payment. Mr. Grant, who had already arranged with his savings and loan company (to whom he owed the $10,000) for a new first mortgage, told the Wards he would make the deal if they would give him a second mortgage for the balance of the down payment. The Wards and Mr. Grant went to an escrow company (in this case, probably, one that was associated with the savings and loan company) and filled out the escrow instructions.

The Wards signed a promissory note for $21,000 in which they agreed to pay the savings and loan company $150 a month, including 7% interest. They also signed a mortgage naming the savings and loan company as mortgagee. Then they signed a second promissory note for $3,000, in which they promised to pay Mr. Grant $30 a month, including 8% interest for seven years, at which time the remaining balance would be due. They also signed a second mortgage naming Mr. Grant as the secondary mortgagee. This mortgage, which had the same fine print as the first mortgage, contained a paragraph stating that it was subject to a prior obligation to the savings and loan company.

Let me emphasize, again, that there were *two* papers (a note and a mortgage) to cover the $21,000 debt and *two* papers (another note and a second mortgage) to cover the $3,000 debt.

The rest of the transaction was very much like the earlier example, except that the Wards got two payment books, one for the first mortgage and one for the second mortgage. The savings and loan company got the $21,000 note, the recorded first mortgage, a title insurance policy, and a copy of the endorsed fire insurance policy naming them as senior mortgagee. Mr. Grant received the $3,000 note, the recorded second mortgage, a copy of the title insurance policy naming him as junior mortgagee, a recorded request for notice (a short paper that named him as junior mortgagee and asked that he be notified in the event of forced sale of the property), and a payment book. Mr. Grant also received a release (or reconveyance) that cleared him of any obligation on his old indebtedness. The final item, of course, was the cash settlement. Mr. Grant received $13,000—the $2,000 down payment and the $11,000 from the savings and loan company (the difference between his old mortgage and the new one).

● THE SECOND MORTGAGE WAS OFFERED FOR SALE

Mr. Grant invested his $13,000 in stocks, which proved so profitable that he was no longer happy with the $30 a month he was getting from that second mortgage. In addition, Mr. Grant, who was the sort of person who hated to keep notifying people that their payments were late, was unhappy to find that the Wards were usually ten to 15 days late. So he took his payment book to a broker and showed him that the Wards, though late, were keeping up the payments and had reduced their debt from $3,000 to $2,800.

"How much can I get for this second mortgage?" he asked the broker. "$2,500?"

The broker shook his head. "You must remember that this is a second mortgage. You'll be lucky to get $2,000."

Mr. Grant did not like that figure, but he was so eager to buy a certain stock that he agreed to let the broker handle it. In the end he sold it at a 30% discount, receiving $1,960 in cash—less the broker's fee.

* * * * * *

We have seen the workings of two transactions that produce mortgages which enter the market as securities that are bought and sold, usually at discounts. Let us now outline a third transaction which produces a rather large number of second mortgages that become available to investors. Again we will use the same names.

● REAL ESTATE BROKERS ACCEPT SECONDS
FOR THEIR COMMISSIONS

Fred Grant owned a house with a first mortgage balance of $19,500. He wanted to sell it at a price that would give him $5,000 in cash for a down payment on another house. He talked it over with a Realtor named Gary White, who pointed out that Grant would have to price the house high enough to cover the sales commission and the transfer fees. Since these costs would come to something like $1,500, White suggested that Grant should price the house at $26,000 and ask for a $6,500 down payment.

John and Mary Ward were willing to pay $26,000 for the house, but they only had $5,000 for the down payment. Mr. Grant refused to sell unless he got $6,500. White, eager to earn his commission on the deal, went to the savings and loan company to see if they would refinance the mortgage at $21,000. They were willing to do this on condition of extra charges and a higher interest rate. But this solution was unacceptable to the Wards, who did not want to pay a higher rate of interest.

White then tried to get Grant to accept $5,000 in cash and a $1,500 second mortgage. Mr. Grant refused. He had to have $6,500 in cash so he could pay the $1,500 sales costs and still have $5,000 for the other house.

"I'll tell you what we'll do," said Mr. White. "We'll have the Wards pay $5,000 in cash. You get that. Then we'll have them sign a $1,500 second mortgage made out to me. That will cover my commission."

"What about the transfer costs?" asked Mr. Grant.

"Suit yourself," said Mr. White. "If you can't spare $100 for the transfer fees, we can drop this deal and wait for someone to come along with $6,500. That may be three months from now."

"All right," agreed Grant. "I guess I can pay those fees."

The deal went through according to White's plan. The Wards

put up their $5,000, agreed to assume the existing first mortgage of $19,500, and signed a $1,500 note and second mortgage that went to Gary White.

Mr. White, however, needed cash for his own day-to-day expenses; so he promptly sold the second mortgage at a 20% discount. The discount cut his commission a little, but he was happy to obtain this lesser sum of money for a completed transaction that might have dragged on for months.

Let us conclude this discussion by pointing out that it doesn't matter what circumstances caused the original mortgagee (Mr. Grant in the first two examples and Mr. White in the third example) to sell his note with attached mortgage. Once the Wards have signed the note, they have created a continuing obligation that can be bought and sold in the same way that the promise of General Motors or United States Steel can be bought and sold. We call the promise of these giant corporations a bond; we call the promise of the Wards a mortgage (even though the primary document is a note). And it is perfectly safe for me—or you—to buy that promissory note with its attached mortgage. The Wards must pay the new mortgagee, to whom the two papers have been transferred by the original mortgagee, or lose their house by foreclosure.

7

I LIKE THE DOUBLE PROTECTION

● TWO DOCUMENTS ARE BETTER
   THAN ONE

In the last chapter, we showed how mortgages originated and how they reached the marketing stage. We will now go back to an important point that was emphasized during those transactions—the fact that two papers are signed by the mortgagor in every mortgage transaction. They are obviously meant as double protection for the mortgagee (the individual or company that sells the property, advances the money, or arranges the sale —and, by extension, any person who acquires the instruments by purchase). They *are* double protection, because different factors stand behind each document. The *credit and good faith* of the debtor back up his signed note, while the *property* stands behind the mortgage.

A person who buys mortgages must be very careful to assess *both* of the factors that stand behind those two papers. Those are the factors that determine the amount of the discount (and the realizable profit for the discounter). If the credit of the home-buyer is unimpeachable and the value of the property is two or three times the amount of the mortgage, the two documents are gilt edged and there would be no discount. If the credit of the home-buyer is nonexistent and the true value of the property is less than the amount of the mortgage, both papers are so worthless that the discount would be fantastically high. But you wouldn't think of trying for the profit promised by the high discount because you would be afraid of losing what money you did pay out. Somewhere, then, between these two extremes, you must find a deal that is both profitable and safe.

Let us discuss this a little more. In the first three chapters of this book, I gave true examples that illustrated the limits that I would go in balancing profits against security on the basis of the factors that stand behind the note and the mortgage. By referring back to the example in the first chapter (the Baker deal), you will note that I was doubtful whether there was full property value as security behind the mortgage. Also, the fact that both of the Bakers were currently employed was no proof of their credit and good faith. However, when Mrs. Baker said she wanted her children to go to the new neighborhood school, I upgraded the factor of credit and good faith. I was willing to risk my money. I was ignoring the mortgage and the real estate security behind it and depending on the note and the factor that stood behind it—that the Bakers would make the payments.

In the example in the second chapter (the Rivera deal), I was able to satisfy myself that both the note and the mortgage had values behind them. The conversation with the old Mexican lady helped me make an appraisal, which indicated that the property value was far above the balance remaining on the mortgage. The personal financial information about the Riveras suggested that their credit and good faith were excellent. I was willing to make an investment at a lower discount which would show less profit.

● BROKERS EMPHASIZE PROPERTY VALUE

When you start to examine mortgages offered for sale, you will find that brokers will emphasize the value of the property and the owner's equity much more than they will talk about the good credit of the note-signer. This is understandable. Brokers do not have time to make thorough credit checks on all the debtors whose mortgages pass through their hands. But they usually know a great deal about property values. In most cases, they have looked at the property and made a quick appraisal. It is only natural for them to emphasize the feature with which they are most familiar.

For my part, I reverse the emphasis, particularly when the transaction involves a second mortgage. It has been my experience that bad credit risks with a considerable equity in their home are as careless about their investment as they are about prompt payments. By the time you pay the delinquency on the first mortgage during the legal redemption period, absorb the foreclosure costs, finance needed repairs on the property, and pay for the expenses of reselling, you may not get as much as you put into the discounted mortgage. The equity—the difference between the total indebtedness and the market value—has evaporated.

● I PUT MY MONEY ON PEOPLE

On the other hand, a couple who are a good credit risk, even if they paid too much for the property, may make all their payments as regular as clockwork. Perhaps, as in the case of the Bakers, the total of their indebtedness was as high as a conservative appraisal of the market value of the house. They really had no equity—and I knew it. But I did not count on the security behind the mortgage. I counted on the note and my belief that they would make the payments. They did—and the correctness of my judgment has proven profitable for me.

This emphasis on the note and the credit and good faith of the signers would suggest that you should always interview the home-buyers. But this does not mean that you should ignore the value of the property that stands behind the mortgage. I always take a look at the property. As a matter of fact, I can think of an example in which one would make an appraisal of the property and never interview the homeowner.

● A FAST DEAL

This is the story. A broker told me he had a small first mortgage at a nominal discount. The note, originally for $10,000, had been paid down to $1,300. It was offered to me for $1,200. With monthly payments of $65, it would pay off in less than two years. I made a quick trip to look at the house—to make sure there was still a house on the lot. I drove by the small house without stopping and returned to the broker's office to tell him I would take the mortgage. With the tenfold security that protected me as I picked up a $100 bill, I wasn't interested in the character of the homeowners. The only time I ever saw those people was when I personally delivered their cancelled note and released mortgage at the end of the period of payments.

● AN INVESTOR CAN MAKE ONE MISTAKE

Before I conclude this chapter, I want to emphasize one point very carefully. You must not make a mistake in judging *both* factors in the same investment purchase. If you misjudge the credit and good faith of the homeowners, you can always recoup your loss by foreclosing on the mortgage and taking over the property. If you misjudge on the property value, the credit and good faith of the homeowners, as they continue their payments, will bring you through. But if you misjudge on both, you're in trouble. You have a bad debt that cannot be covered by foreclosure.

Thus, it would be wise to make your first mortgage investment on a deal with a low discount, which has excellent credit behind the note and dependable property value behind the mortgage.

8

HOW TO ASSESS
THE VALUE OF SEASONING

● MORTGAGES FOR SALE

1st mtg. $11,000. $126 per mo. 7% int. Seasoned. Discount.

Seasoned 2nd. $2,900. 20% discount. 10% int. Brkr.

$9,100 1st mtg. $101 per mo. 9%. Will take $7,500. Gd. pay. Brkr.

$1,200 disc. on seasoned $3,580 2nd. 8% int. $38 per mo. Nice home. Due 4 years.

These listings appeared under the heading, "Mortgages for Sale," in the classified section of a newspaper. You will note that three of the four included the word "seasoned," a term I have used without explaining its meaning. This term also appeared in one of the items of the broker's list presented earlier. By this time, therefore, you will be thinking that "seasoned" must be a feature that makes a mortgage more attractive to a buyer. You are right. It does. And you should know why.

If you have already assumed that "seasoned" means "aging," you are correct. The word, as used by real estate dealers and mortgage people, tells you the mortgage is not a new instrument being offered directly after the real estate transaction that created it. It has been in existence for a period of time, payments have been made, and the indicated total of debt is lower than the original loan.

● THE OLDER IT IS, THE BETTER IT IS

This is very important. As any Realtor will tell you, a mortgage is an investment that gets better as it gets older. Every monthly payment reduces the debt and increases the equity of the owner. The ratio of debt to property value drops steadily—which means that the security behind the mortgage becomes relatively greater.

Seasoning also suggests another favorable factor. It tells you that the homeowner has been making his monthly payments regularly. It would follow, apparently, that he will continue to make those regular payments.

All right, having now established that seasoning improves a mortgage, let's jump in and really analyze this so-called advantage.

● IT TAKES MORE THAN A FEW MONTHS

The first question to ask is this: How long have the payments been made? A great many brokers will call a mortgage seasoned as soon as one payment has been made. They rationalize their use of the term by arguing that they want to point out that the offered investment is not a purchase-money mortgage coming on the market directly out of the sale of the property. However, the potential buyer should not consider a mortgage seasoned when it has been in existence only a few months.

Many second mortgages, which are set up on the traditional 1% monthly pay-back, specify the degree of seasoning *right in the advertisement.* Suppose the broker offers an 8% mortgage with a balance of $2,959 and adds the magic word, "seasoned." I can tell you this was originally a $3,000 mortgage on which the monthly payments are $30 and it has been "seasoned" for exactly four months. Get out your pencil and figure it out for yourself.

There is another kind of "seasoned" mortgage which you must consider with a suspicious eye. This is the mortgage in which the monthly installment does not appreciably reduce the balance due. I will give you two examples.

● THE PAYMENT WAS TOO LOW

John Ferguson sold his house with a low down payment and

took back a $3,000 second mortgage with a 7% interest rate. Since he knew that the buyers, Mr. and Mrs. Stewart, were on a tight budget, he cooperated by agreeing to a monthly payment of only $20 a month. A year later, with the balance down to $2,969, he offered it for sale as a seasoned mortgage. He priced it at $2,500. Henry Green, seeing a chance to make over $400, bought it and began to collect $20 a month. As the Stewarts were always late in making their payments, Mr. Green was constantly worried about the danger that he might have to foreclose. He consoled himself with the thought that the Stewart's equity was increasing every month.

When Mr. Green had collected the payments for two and a half years, the Stewarts defaulted. Mr. Green, looking at a balance that was still $2,891, realized that he had only collected $78 on the principal. His security, on the basis of the low pay-back on the second mortgage, had not really increased.

● THE HOUSE WAS OVERPRICED

Here's the second example. Peter Barnes sold his house to the Wilsons. Since the Wilsons were young and inexperienced, and were very eager to buy this particular house, they did not go in for hard bargaining. Barnes was able to sell the house at a price far above the market. But the first mortgage appraisers wouldn't go for such a high figure. They made their loan on the basis of the true market value, which forced Barnes to carry back a $5,000 second mortgage with monthly payments at the traditional 1%— $50 a month. Knowing the whole deal was overpriced, Barnes set the interest rate at 10%—to make the second mortgage more attractive and allow him to sell it as soon as possible. In a few months, he sold the second mortgage at a 25% discount to Mr. Fish. Early in the third year, when the Wilsons had only reduced the $5,000 second mortgage by $270, Mr. Fish had to take over a house that wasn't really worth as much as the first and second mortgages. Mr. Fish managed to resell the house and recover $2,000 of his $3,700 investment.

Both Mr. Green and Mr. Fish learned, the hard way, that true seasoning means something more than time. It means a ratio of interest and monthly payments that have been set to pay off a part of the principal and that will continue to pay off the debt at a reasonably rapid rate.

● TRUE SEASONING

If you will refer back to my example of the $1,300 mortgage in

Chapter 7, you will discover what a truly well-seasoned mortgage means. But there are not many opportunities like that. When a mortgage gets to the last stages of payoff, with a balance that is only a fraction of the property value, the mortgage holder is not apt to sell it. If he does put it on the market, the discount will be so small that there is little profit for the discounter.

● THE OTHER SIDE OF THE PICTURE

Now that you have been convinced of the importance of seasoning, I want to do a complete switch and tell you that there are situations where an unseasoned mortgage may be safer than one that is seasoned. This apparent contradiction can be found in some cases when we dig a little deeper to consider the motive of the mortgage holder who is offering the mortgage for sale.

It should be obvious that there are only two primary motives for selling a mortgage. The holder wants cash or he wants to get rid of his mortgage because there's something wrong with it.

● THE SELLER WANTS CASH

Let us start by considering an unseasoned mortgage that is offered for sale. Barring the few cases where the holder knows that the property was overpriced and those possibly collusive cases where he knows the homeowner will not make the required payments, that mortgagee is selling his mortgage because he wants cash. It is unlikely that he is trying to get rid of a bad investment—because he hasn't had time to find out what kind of debtor the new homeowner will be. It follows, therefore, that such an unseasoned mortgage (except for the overpriced property and the fraudulent deals) need not be suspect simply because the seller is willing to accept a discounted price. If your judgment with respect to the value of the property and the credit and good faith of the homeowner is sound, you can buy such unseasoned mortgages with perfect safety.

● THERE IS SOMETHING WRONG

But you must always consider the motive of the seller who is willing to accept a discount for a mortgage that has been partially seasoned. In this situation, you will find a higher proportion of sellers who want to get rid of their mortgages for various reasons other than a need for cash. The homeowner may be slow to pay, he may be delinquent, there may be domestic problems, the property may have deteriorated, the character of the district may have changed for the worse, it may even be what we call an out-and-out "foreclosure deal." Thus, when you consider a seasoned mortgage, you must do a little detective work to try to determine whether the seller's motive is "cashing out" or "dumping a bad one."

Sometimes you can study a broker's list of offerings and pick out the deals where the seller is trying to move an unsafe or doubtful mortgage. The discount may be too high; the last indicated installment payment may suggest delinquency; the taxes may be unpaid; the location may be in a deteriorating, low-income area; the original down payment may have been too low. So you cross these off at once. Among the remaining offers there will be others that the sellers are anxious to unload. Watch out for them.

● PART OF THE HOUSE WAS MISSING

Let me tell you about a suspicious deal I encountered. The house was a two-bedroom stucco in a working-class suburb, with a $12,000 first mortgage (paid down from $12,500) and a $2,300 second (paid down from $2,500). The property had sold for $16,500 with $1,500 down. I was offered the second mortgage as a seasoned investment at a 20% discount.

I drove out to investigate the proposition and found the owner at home. As I spoke to him at his open front door, I noticed, beyond the living room, that the kitchen seemed to extend into vacant space at the rear of the house.

"Are you remodeling the kitchen?" I asked.

"Come in," said the homeowner, "I'll show you what I'm doing."

I walked in and discovered that a part of the rear house wall had been dismantled, the slab on which the building stood had been extended about 12 feet, and the framework of a new rear wall had been erected. This rear portion of the house, though roofed and enclosed, was only an empty shell.

"With all my kids," said the owner, "I needed more room. So I tore out the back wall and made the house larger. I'm going to move the kitchen back here and put in two more bedrooms and another bathroom."

"There's still a lot to do," I said.

"I keep working on it. Little by little I'll get it done."

I listened and looked as the owner bustled about, showing me the crated bathtub he had already purchased, stepping off the future rooms, going through the motions of installing walls, wiring, plumbing. After this inspection of a house to be, I extended my visit to get all the information available on the homeowner's plans, family, and job—because by now I knew only too well why the former mortgagee wanted to sell his note and mortgage. In its present condition, the property value had dropped from $16,500 to about $13,000 or $14,000. The security behind that second mortgage had virtually disappeared.

I did a lot of thinking as I drove home. The homeowner looked all right as a credit risk. But I didn't want to take over the shell of a house on foreclosure that would require several thousand dollars to make it marketable. On the other hand, if all the improvements were completed, there would be added security. It would be a house worth $20,000. Then I recalled the homeowner's genuine enthusiasm during my tour of inspection. I decided to gamble. I bought that mortgage; and then sweated it out for over a year as the remodeling proceeded, little by little. But that homeowner finally completed his project. Now there is a $20,000 property behind an $11,500 first mortgage and my $1,700 second mortgage.

● THE HEIRS WANT CASH

There is one source of what could truly be considered seasoned mortgages. No one raises any questions about the motives of the former mortgagee because he has left the arena of scheming, investment switching, or cashing out doubtful mortgages—he is dead.

Upon the death of a mortgage holder, his widow or children may keep the mortgage as an income-producing security. More often, however, the estate must be divided between a number of heirs. In this case, the executor will seek to convert the mortgage into cash by putting it up for sale on an open-bid basis.

These probate mortgages can generally be purchased at very decent discounts. As with all good things, however, there is a catch in it. The potential buyer has to make his bid without knowing whether he is going to be the successful purchaser. But, once he has decided to bid, he must tie up some money in a down payment and make sure he will have the balance of the money on hand at an unknown time in the near future. As a result, he keeps a considerable sum of money idle during the weeks and months of probate delays. In the end, as occasionally happens, he may be outbid at what may be virtually a second auction, because the probate judge will entertain any offer substantially higher than his at the final court hearing for confirmation of his previously accepted high bid. These factors are so aggravating that there are many mortgage discounters who will not even try for probate mortgages.

Some investors, however, are willing to suffer the delays and disappointments to buy these relatively safe mortgages. And you may wish to be one of those investors. If so, you will have to learn how to go about the business of buying them.

● HOW AND WHERE TO FIND PROBATE MORTGAGES

You may be able to get them through a broker who specializes in mortgages—perhaps the same broker who is already sending you lists of offers. He watches the notices of such probate sales, and he is also notified by the attorneys who handle probate cases containing estate mortgages. If a probate mortgage appears on a broker's list, there may be a tentative discount suggested by him on the basis of the quality of the mortgage and the state of the money market. However, you may alter that discount offer by proposing a figure higher or lower than that suggested by the broker. You can talk this over with him, and he will probably also explain that you may not be the successful bidder.

You can watch the advertisements in legal newspapers. Since the sale of estate property must be advertised, mortgages will appear under the probate heading, "Personal Property to be Sold at Private Sale," and it will be listed as "a promissory note secured by real property." In addition to being advertised in legal newspapers, these "secured notes" will be offered for sale through public posting. You can ask someone in your county courthouse about such postings of estate property offered for sale in probate proceedings.

● PAYMENT PATTERNS

There is one final item about seasoning that may be helpful, though it may be a decisive factor in only a fraction of the offers you consider.

Since people are creatures of habit, they generally carry out repeated actions in much the same way. We could call this an established pattern of behavior. Thus, homeowners follow a certain pattern in making their installment payments. A debtor, who generally pays on time, will continue the process. One who pays ten days late will usually continue to be ten days late. The one who is constantly a month or more late will continue to be very late. In addition to these, there are the variables—the ones whose payments are ahead of time one month and very late at the next payment date.

If you can talk to the former mortgagee (or look at the payment book), you will know what to expect as a pattern of payment. And you will be forewarned. If you are the type of person who makes all your own payments promptly, the late payment pattern may cause you so much distress that you might be better off if you refused to buy any mortgage where the debtor is always late. Most mortgage investors, however, are realistic about what can be expected of a homeowner. As long as the payment pattern is not unreasonably bad, they are prepared for the pattern of payments that a seasoned mortgage exhibits, and they adjust their own collection procedure to the known situation.

As for the variable payers, this calls for an examination that may lead to a perfectly logical explanation, or one that may cause you to drop the deal as if it were a live bomb.

9

JUDGING THE SAFETY OF YOUR MORTGAGE INVESTMENT

From the experiences I have already reported, you should have gleaned some ideas about the safety of the mortgages which appear on the market. The remainder of the book will give you many more. However, it may be helpful if we present a comprehensive discussion, in one chapter, about the information you need to help judge the value of the security behind the mortgage and the financial dependability of the homeowner-debtor.

● WE ARE BUYING EXISTING MORTGAGES

As we open this discussion, I want to remind you that this is not a book about loaning money to a homeowner who needs financial assistance. We are not making the original loan; we are buying a mortgage that is already in existence or, in the case of hard-money seconds, we are agreeing to provide the money on a mortgage arranged by someone else.

64

This means that someone else has already appraised the property and judged the financial situation of the homeowner-debtor. Our job, therefore, is to pass judgment on that previous investigation. Some investors, if they are meticulously legalistic and overly cautious, will want to do the entire investigation all over again. They will require an appraisal by a professional expert to establish the precise value of the property on the basis of the size of the lot, the square feet in the house, the quality of the plumbing fixtures, the number of closets, etc—plus such factors as the character of the neighborhood and the going price for similar homes. They will want a complete credit report on the homeowner.

I am very much in favor of this careful analysis. In practice, however, you cannot use this approach on deals where it is readily apparent that they are safe and profitable. There isn't time.

If a mortgage is a good one, providing both security and high yield, it will be snapped up before a cautious buyer can begin to get his investigative machinery in operation. As a result, the cautious buyer will always be left in a position of judging doubtful or dangerous mortgage offers. Why? Because the best ones have already been taken by experienced investors who have learned how important it is to make quick decisions.

Let us assume that you are the cautious buyer. You receive a list of mortgage offerings in the Thursday mail. You go over the list and choose a seasoned first mortgage with a balance of $11,400. The monthly payment is $145, including 7% interest. The discount is 15%.

On Friday you visit the property. The homeowner's wife, alone in the house, will not let you in to look at it. However, she does tell you that they have always been prompt with their payments; she is willing to tell you where her husband works and when he will be home. Although you are not sure an appraiser will be allowed into the house, you arrange for a professional appraisal on Monday. You also call a local credit bureau to request a credit report on that homeowner. On Monday afternoon, satisfied with your reports, you call the broker to tell him you want to buy that mortgage.

It's too late. He has already sold it to me.

● QUICK ACTION

This is what I did. Having chosen this offering from the list that arrived in my Thursday mail, I quickly figured the yield—a fraction more than 11%. Then I called the broker, obtained every bit of information that he could give me, and asked him to hold it for me until noon of the following day.

In the afternoon, accompanied by my wife, I drove out to look at the house. After cruising the immediate neighborhood to estimate the quality and market price of these moderately valued homes, I parked in front of the house. My wife and I discussed its appearance and probable value. Then I got out and walked up the street to make a careful survey of the other houses in the block. On my return, I casually paced off the frontage of the house and multiplied it with an estimate of the depth to get the square footage.

I went to the door and explained the purpose of my visit to the homeowner's wife, adding the information that my wife was waiting in my car. When she made no move to suggest that my wife should join us, I told her I seldom bothered about an inspection of the house interior. However, I added, I did want to know the number of bedrooms and baths. She answered that question and confirmed my information about the original down payment and the years they had owned the house. I asked about schools, and we were soon talking about her two children. She told me her husband's occupation, where he worked, and his approximate seniority.

In the evening, my wife and I discussed the deal and decided it was satisfactory. The following morning, as soon as the recorder's office was open, I was there to look at the microfilm of the original mortgage (from which I copied the legal description). After checking the files to see that there had been no liens or claims against the property, I went to the map department and took a look at the survey plat of the original subdivision. I then drove over to the broker's office and told him I would buy the mortgage.

The foregoing is a fictitious account—but the speed of my investigation and decision is not exaggerated. On such a secure first mortgage, you have to act fast. Witness a true occurrence that happened the other day: Gardner obtained a mortgage listing at noon and began to call his clients. My wife reported that he called me about 3:00 PM. I was out and did not return until after his office was closed. When I called him back the following morning, I was told that the mortgage had been sold.

● WHAT YOU SHOULD KNOW

Now that I have impressed you with the necessity for rapid investigation, let us slow down a little and consider what you should know about appraising the homeowner's residence and financial situation.

In the first place, you may as well forget about obtaining a professional appraisal. There isn't time; the homeowner (who is not asking for a loan) will seldom allow your appraiser inside his house;

and you *already have a report of its market value*—because the house was sold at a certain price, with a specified down payment, a first mortgage of "X" dollars, and perhaps a second mortgage of "Z" dollars.

Nevertheless, you do want to know many things about the home-owner, the mortgage, and as much as possible about the property. Here is a list of the information you should try to obtain:

A Checklist

1. Name and address of broker.

2. Name and address of mortgage holder (seller).

3. Type of house.

4. Address of property.

5. Legal description of property.

6. Lot size.

7. Name and telephone number of homeowner.

8. Employer; salary; seniority; business telephone.

9. Does wife work?

10. Wife's employer; salary; seniority; business telephone.

11. Children.

12. Date of purchase.

13. Purchase price.

14. Down payment.

15. Amount of original first mortgage; interest rate; monthly payment.

16. Present balance of first mortgage.

17. F. H. A. or V. A. (G. I.) ?

18. Acceleration clause; prepayment penalty.

19. Due date.

20. Amount of discount.

21. Why is mortgage holder selling? (Don't expect a truthful answer.)

22. Area where house is located.

23. Nearest important street.

24. Level lot; hillside; view?

25. Zoning classification.

26. Condition of grounds and driveway.

27. Garage or carport—size, location, construction.

28. Cars owned.

29. Age of house.

30. Type of construction.

31. Condition of paint, window screens, storm windows.

32. Basement; heating system.

33. Type of roof—condition.

34. Pool; patio; barbecue.

35. Exterior size of house.

36. Number of bedrooms; bathrooms.

37. Layout of house—stories?

38. Family room; service room.

39. Built-ins; carpeting.

40. Amount of taxes—delinquent or current?

41. Special assessments.

42. Assessed value on tax rolls.

43. Unusual features; personal notes.

Additional Items for Second Mortgage Deal

1. Lender on first mortgage.

2. First mortgage loan number.

3. Was second a hard-money or purchase-money mortgage?

4. Reason for second.

5. Original amount; interest rate; monthly payment.

6. Date of inception of second.

7. Present balance.

8. Acceleration clause; prepayment penalty.

9. Due date.

10. Amount of discount.

11. Is discount negotiable?

12. Unusual features; personal notes.

● DON'T EXPECT TO GET ALL THE ANSWERS

You will not get information on all those items. However, if you make use of all possible sources of information—former mortgage holder, broker, talkative children, a roomer or relative, neighbors, recorder's office, homeowners' employers—you will be surprised at how much information you can pick up.

If you have too many blanks on your checklist, extend your visit at the homeowner's house and try to keep the conversation going. People like to talk about themselves. Listen carefully, but do not take notes. You may shut off the flow of information. (When you get to your car, you can fill out your checklist.)

Keep your eyes and ears open for the unusual hint or comment to put after number 43 (or number 12 of the Additional Items list). It may be the single important item you need to tell you how to make the right decision.

● I TAKE SOMEONE ALONG

Whenever possible, I ask my wife, a friend, or one of my daughters to accompany me on inspection trips. Two sets of eyes are better than one. While I am looking at the roof, my wife can spot the trash behind the bushes at the side of the house. While I am stepping off the size of the house, my daughter can strike up a conversation with the inquisitive neighbor next door.

In one case, I turned down a deal because my daughter called my attention to the absence of an essential retaining wall. In another case, my wife pointed out that the house was too isolated.

● THE HOMEOWNER'S CREDIT

I am definitely sorry that I can't get a good assessment of the homeowner's financial condition—one that will guarantee that he will make every payment until the mortgage is paid off. I don't have access to reports from a credit bureau; I don't have time to make the kind of thorough personal checkup I would prefer. So I have to console myself with the fact that I do have considerable information.

I know that the homeowner has made a down payment of "X"

number of dollars. I know that he has made regular payments for a certain length of time, and I make a special effort to find out if those payments were prompt or slow. I always ask whether the homeowner's wife is employed. I consider it important to know the homeowner's job rating, seniority, and length of time on the job. You can be sure that I am alert to any possible hint that will tell me whether these people are thrifty or extravagant.

In the end, however, I probably make my judgment on the basis of a combination of the *absence* of any warning indication of irresponsibility and the *"feel"* that the homeowners are people of character and dependability. I usually do as well as the mortgage investor who obtains a complete credit report. After all, neither of us can really be certain what the future will bring.

Checking the Legal Description

In Chapter 13, A Checklist for Your Documents, you will find considerable emphasis on the careful checking of the legal description to insure that it reads precisely the same on all the documents. But there is an important task for you to perform before you reach the stage of the actual purchase of the mortgage. You must be certain that the legal description does, in fact, refer to the property which you are investigating at a certain street address.

Let us suppose you are offered a mortgage on a house at 1542 S. Phillips Street. You make your investigation and decide to buy it. At this point you stop buying a mortgage on a property at 1542 S. Phillips Street and begin to buy one on a parcel of improved real estate known as Lot 7 of Block 12 of the Bourne Tract. When the transaction is completed, your investment will not be secured by 1542 S. Phillips Street; it will be secured by Lot 7 of Block 12 of the Bourne Tract. You must be absolutely certain that the street address and the legal description are one and the same property.

This is how I check this essential point. I go to the map department in the recorder's office and look at the photocopy of the survey of the Bourne Tract. I see that the Bourne Tract is 12 square blocks between 13th and 16th, east of Phillips Street. I note that Block 12 is the block between 15th and 16th, and that Lot 7 is the seventh lot south of 15th and the third lot north of 16th. I recall my visit to 1542 S. Phillips Street and decide that the legal description does tally with the street address, because the house I inspected was the third from the corner of 16th. If I want to be absolutely certain, however, I look at the lot frontages shown on the survey and note that the southeast corner of Lot 7 is 100 feet from 16th Street. Then I make a second trip out to Phillips Street to confirm that the southwest corner of the property at 1542 is 33 paces from 16th Street.

The reason I am so meticulous is because I have had two close calls. In the first case, I found myself with a mortgage on a house next door to the one I had intended to buy. (This was a clerical error by the title insurance company, which was corrected.) In the other case, I was offered a mortgage on a corner house with the legal description of an identical corner house three blocks away. What's more, the homeowner and the former owner both had incorrect grant deeds, which meant that two successive homeowners had been living in a house they didn't own. Needless to say, I didn't buy that mortgage.

10

A LOW-PRICED MORTGAGE
FOR MY DAUGHTER

● FOR THE SMALLEST INVESTOR

If you have saved a little money, I'm sure you've experienced the frustration of the small operator in the field of finance. You don't have enough to buy 100 shares of a good stock; you don't have enough to buy into a good business; you can't buy income property; and you must be saying, "I don't have enough to buy mortgages." But you are wrong. You can—especially if you have good credit or some sort of financial backing.

This is the story of a mortgage purchase in which the buyer had only $150.

In the midst of a sudden uprush of my mortgage activity—good offers from several sources, investigations of properties, conferences with my banker, and calculations of my cash flow—my high school daughter reported that she had to work on a semester project for her "General Business" course. I suggested that she do a report on a mortgage transaction,

72

explaining that I could provide her with documents that would fill out her project. She sat down with me and listened to my explanation of deeds, notes, mortgages, and escrows. Since she had already soaked up a little information about my business activities, she was soon in command of the whole process.

● A SCHOOL PROJECT LEADS TO A REAL PROJECT

She gathered up blank documents and prepared a folder containing everything involved in a mortgage purchase—the broker's mimeographed listing of offered mortgages, escrow instructions, note, mortgage, assignment, title policy, request for notice, offset statement, and payment book. She did such a thorough job that I was not surprised when she came home to tell me that her project report made a tremendous impression on her teacher. But I was not prepared for the final outcome of this school activity. My daughter wanted to go into such a transaction—for real!

"You don't have enough money," I told her.

"I have a savings account," she replied.

"With $100 in it," I scoffed.

"A hundred and fifty," she corrected me. "And I could borrow some money from Betty. She has a lot of money in the bank."

I shook my head. "You have to have at least $1,000."

"Maybe I could borrow some money from Ann." (Ann is her older married sister.)

I shook my head decisively. This type of investment was not for a 16-year-old girl who had to scrape up money from school friends and relatives.

Six months later, one of my small second mortgages with a balance of $800 came due. Platt, the owner of the house, a rental property near his home, asked for a new loan of $1,200. Knowing his situation and his payment record, I could have agreed to this new loan, which would be a 10% hard-money deal. But I had another, larger discount transaction on the fire. I told him I didn't want to renew his mortgage nor advance any additional money.

In a few days, Platt called me back to ask me if I would renew the $800. He had discovered, in a tight money situation, that it would cost over $200 in fees to get a new $1,000 second mortgage.

"I won't renew the old mortgage," I told him. "But I may be able to find someone to make a new loan. I'll let you know in a few days."

● GATHERING UP THE LOOSE CHANGE

The "someone" I had in mind was my daughter. I proposed that she should borrow $250 at 6% from her older sister (who was getting 5% for her savings). I would then loan her the $800 Platt still owed, also at 6%, and she could put in her $150. This would make the $1,200 Platt had originally requested, all at 10%.

To my surprise, she didn't jump at this chance to get into the mortgage business. First we had to figure all the interest—the monthly cost of the borrowed money at 6% and the monthly return from Mr. Platt at 10%.

"I won't make very much," she complained, "only $4 a month."

"That's a lot more than you get from the bank," I said.

"What if he doesn't make the payments?" she worried.

"You foreclose."

"What will that cost?"

"A couple of hundred. And, of course, you will have to make the payments on the first mortgage," I warned her.

"How much are the payments on the first?"

"Seventy-four dollars a month."

She was scared. This business of loaning money on a second mortgage was dangerous. She didn't like it.

● A LITTLE BACKING HELPS

I reassured her, promising to put up the money for foreclosure costs and first mortgage payments if Platt didn't keep up his payments.

"After those costs are out of the way," I told her, "you would have a nice little house that rents for $100 a month."

She did some more figuring on the basis of being a landlady.

"All right," she agreed, "I'll call Ann to see if she'll loan me the $250."

I took her out to see the house, a two-bedroom stucco that was worth at least $14,000. Then we called on Platt and listened to a report on his financial problems. (It looked to me as if he was in a better situation than when I had first bought his second mortgage.) He gave us the exact amount of his first mortgage balance ($10,000) and explained that he was now getting $110 rent from a dependable tenant.

I told him that the new mortgage would name me and my daughter, in joint tenancy, as the mortgagees; that we could bypass the escrow expenses, if he would permit me to hold two notes (the old and the new) until the papers were recorded; and that I would charge only $25 to cover the recording fees, transfer of funds, postage, and car expense. This cost was such a small amount, when compared with normal loan fees, that Mr. Platt was delighted. He and his wife signed the new note and mortgage and I gave him a check for the difference between the old balance and the new loan—less the $25. After releasing the old mortgage and having the release recorded and sent to him, I mailed him the old note marked "Paid in Full." I recorded the new mortgage and had it mailed to my daughter. In the meantime, she had signed a $250 note for her sister and an $800 note for me. Then she gave me the $400. She was now in business.

● SHE WANTS ANOTHER MORTGAGE

My daughter has been collecting $20 a month for several years, she has reimbursed her sister, and has paid off part of her debt to me. Now, graduated from high school and working at a full-time job, with money in the bank, she wants to buy another mortgage. But she is quite sharp about this business. She doesn't want another hard-money mortgage. She wants to get the discount on a purchase-money mortgage.

I think we'll soon find another small, seasoned second mortgage that she can buy because there are always a few small seconds coming into the market. And they can be bought at good discounts. There is a perfectly good reason for this supply of small mortgages: Most professional mortgage investors do not care to buy small seconds because the monthly payments are often somewhere between $12 and $18. Yet it costs just as much, in postage and collection expense, to service a small mortgage as it does a bigger one.

Thus, for the beginner, there are small mortgages to be bought. *There is an opportunity to get into a profitable investment field with a limited amount of capital.*

11

I SELDOM BUY HARD-MONEY SECOND MORTGAGES

● AN OLD-FASHIONED MORTGAGE

In a sense, my daughter invested in a hard-money second mortgage. Since I have mentioned this type of mortgage —and will be referring to them again— we had better present a fairly complete discussion of hard-money mortgages.

Strictly speaking, a hard-money mortgage is an old-fashioned mortgage, the kind that was in existence long before the days when mortgages became a part of a transaction in which homes were bought on the installment plan.

A property owner needed money. To obtain it, he signed a promissory note and pledged his property as a guarantee that he would repay the debt. You will note that he did not acquire possession of a home in this deal; he already owned that home. What he got for his mortgage was cash. Hence, the name "hard money."

After the introduction of purchase-money mortgages as a means to buy

76

homes, the present-day hard-money second mortgages appeared. Homeowners, buying a house on payments, now had an increasing equity in a parcel of real estate. As persons of property, even if it was only a portion of the value of a house, they could borrow money at a rate lower than that charged by pawnbrokers or small-loan companies. Lenders, seeing that their loans were protected by pledged real estate, were willing to advance cash at a rate much higher than they could obtain from an institutional savings account.

● THE HOME MORTGAGE COMPANY

But someone had to bring the potential borrowers and lenders together. This role was filled by a very specialized kind of brokerage concern which came to be known as a home mortgage company or a home loan company. (The customary terms of reference were unfortunate because it suggested that they loaned out money which investors deposited with them. But they did not operate in this manner. They were loan brokers, arranging loans that each individual investor made to each individual borrower.)

These firms obtained their operating income from commissions and fees, which were paid by the borrower at the time he obtained the loan. This payment was not in the form of a check drawn on the borrower's bank account, of course; it was a deduction from the money advanced by the lender. The hard money that the borrower received, therefore, was always somewhat less than the face amount of his note and second mortgage.

● THE BORROWER

Let's explain the whole transaction with an example. Peter Brendan was buying a $20,000 house on which he had made a $3,500 down payment. Some years later, when his original $16,500 first mortgage had been reduced to $15,000, he encountered a financial emergency that required $1,000. He answered the newspaper advertisement of the Carter Company, a home loan firm, and explained his needs. After he filled out a loan application, the Carter Company sent an appraiser out to value his home. Since property values had risen, the market price was set at $21,000 and Mr. Brendan's equity was calculated to be $6,000. The Carter Company, operating on a conservative basis of limiting the homeowner's total indebtedness to 80% of the market value of his property, figured there was an $1,800 loan value between the existing

$15,000 debt and the 80% figure of $16,800. Since this was well above the $1,400 second mortgage that was being considered, they agreed to arrange the loan.

● THE LENDER

Arthur Marpell, who sometimes invested small amounts in hard-money second mortgages, was pleased at the growth of his savings account. On the morning that the list of offerings from the Carter Company arrived, his savings had reached $2,400. So he was interested in the proposed Brendan loan. He saw that he could invest the required amount and still keep $1,000 as a cash reserve. He studied the fairly long report on Brendan's property, job, first mortgage, and family status. He considered the payment plan—which was to be $25 a month, including 10% interest, with a due date of three years, at which time there would be a final balloon payment of about $840. Then he went out and looked at Brendan's house—a well-kept home that looked as if it should be worth $21,000. He promptly called the Carter Company and told them he would advance the $1,400.

The Carter Company arranged all the details of the transaction. In due course they sent Marpell the note, recorded second mortgage, title insurance policy, and other essential documents. They sent Brendan a statement of their commission and fees, which came to $350, and a check for the net proceeds—$1,050. Then they set up a ledger account and file on the Brendan loan, because Marpell had authorized them to handle Brendan's monthly payments, a service the Carter Company provided for their investor clients without charge.

This transaction is duplicated again and again—because it is an attractive and well-advertised activity. Furthermore, investments in hard-money second mortgages will almost meet the profit specifications of my book title—a 10% return will double your money in about seven years.

● FOR THE BUSY PERSON

For a person who is very busy at his regular occupation, or one who does not have the temperament or judgment to carry out the investigations and negotiations required for discount operations, it might be sensible to concentrate on hard-money seconds. Although not as spectacular as the stock market, where a favorable news item can give you a quick profit and a sneeze in the White House can wipe out your life savings, hard-money second mortgages pay well and have the security of a piece of property to protect them.

● YOU SHOULD CONSIDER HOW FINANCIAL INSTITUTIONS OPERATE

Before I proceed to list the advantages of hard-money seconds, let me express my amazement at the thousands of hard-working, economical savers who run from one savings institution to another in pursuit of an additional fraction of a per cent. They are happy to have $5,000 on deposit at 5%.

Perhaps they are happy because they believe their money is locked up every night in a massive vault. However, they know that isn't true. Money in a safe never earned anything for anyone. Perhaps they are happy because they have been told that their account is backed by billions in assets. But no one ever mentions the billions of liabilities; nor do they tell you that the assets are thousands and thousands of promissory notes—the notes of debtors who are using the depositor's money for everything from a television set to a jet airplane. Perhaps they are impressed by the size of the building, the paintings on the wall of the lobby, or the friendly smile of the teller.

Whatever the reason, I shall continue to be amazed and the savers will probably continue drawing their quarterly 5% interest payments.

● ADVANTAGES OF HARD-MONEY SECONDS

Here, in brief, are some of the advantages of investing in the hard-money second mortgages that you can purchase from a home mortgage company. You will receive an interest rate of 10% or more, paid every month. (Your monthly check will actually be more, because that monthly payment includes part of the principal.) Your money will not be tied up too long because these hard-money seconds are usually arranged for a three-year period. You will have the promissory note and second mortgage, a tangible documentary asset that you can see. Collections will be handled for you by the home mortgage company, and, in the event of delinquency, the follow-up procedure will be experienced and effective.

If you are dealing with a dependable home mortgage company, you can be sure that they have checked out the two factors that stand behind the loan—before they agreed to offer it for sale. They have made a credit check of the homeowner which is more extensive than the inquiries I generally make. They have appraised the property and limited the loan to a size that should promise an even break (or more) for the investor in the event of default, foreclosure, and resale.

At this point, when we refer to the possibility of default, I would like to mention an important point. Established home mortgage companies will always be on the side of the investor, conferring with him at every step of a delinquent mortgage situation, because they must maintain their reputation with their investors to keep a clientele of people who have money to lend. While they will be courteous and helpful to the homeowner who wants to borrow money, they will not relax their strict loan collection program to retain the goodwill of a homeowner-debtor. For every debtor customer they lose, there will be five to take his place in the waiting room of the home mortgage office. (In times of easy money, of course, there is the possibility that this situation could reverse itself. In that event, with the debtor being coddled, investors must be on their guard for bad paper.)

● DON'T ASK YOUR FRIENDS

If you think the preceding account was a glowing prospectus for hard-money second mortgages, you should recall one important item—the requirement that the home mortgage company should be well established and dependable. This leads to the question: How does a beginning investor determine which home mortgage firm fits that description? I will answer that with a statement that may surprise you: Do not choose the home mortgage company *solely* on the basis of the recommendation of friends or acquaintances.

This is the snare that has trapped unwary investors again and again. A group of sharp operators in anything from stamps to securities can set up an imposing office and secure the investment funds of a few people for their particular get-rich-quick project. They then pay out (from the investment funds deposited) fantastically high returns. The first investors, happy with these quick results, spread the good word to their friends. Everyone rushes to put their money into the hands of these confidence men—who now have even more money, to pay out ever larger payments. People flood into the office, clamoring to invest their money.

It now becomes unnecessary to pay out the 20% profit in cash. The first timid investors, reinforced by the paper profits that everyone seems to be getting, bring back their profits (or dividends or interest) for reinvestment. Everything is wonderful; everyone is making money. If you don't believe it, ask your friend who has invested his money. He will know more about the firm's operations than the original promoters. When the haul becomes large enough —or the authorities begin to investigate—the whole deal collapses and the unhappy investor is lucky if he gets a few cents back for every dollar he deposited.

● YOU HAVE TO CHECK THEM OUT YOURSELF

So much for the negative side, which is not intended to reflect on any home mortgage company. Most of them are perfectly safe, and the most dependable can be determined by your own efforts.

Let us say that a friend recommends a certain home mortgage company. If he has been doing business with them for several years, his recommendation is valuable. Your second step is to talk to an official of the company. Ask him for an honest report on the worst possible outcome of your potential investment—the case when the debtor defaults and the investor is required to advance the payments on the first mortgage and foreclose. A dependable company will not hide the fact that a small percentage of their loans do go sour. (The percentage is very small.) Ask the mortgage company representative about bonding arrangements to protect you during the purchase transaction. A dependable concern will be more than happy to explain, carefully, just how they take care of this problem.

Your next step is to choose one of the company's recommended loan offers and make a thorough inspection on your own. Interview the homeowner—at length—and make your own careful appraisal of his house. Call the savings and loan company to confirm the facts about the first mortgage. If you find everything to be as represented, you should have some confidence in that home mortgage company. Buy the second mortgage. Repeat this field investigation on a later purchase. By the time of a third purchase, you should be convinced that the firm is dependable. You can relax.

● I MAKE MORE MONEY BY DISCOUNTING

I do not ordinarily buy hard-money second mortgages. If you will go back and reread Chapter 1 and Chapter 4, you will find the reason for that opening statement. I can make more money (in total yield) by buying mortgages at a discount. In California, where state law restricts the rate of interest on real estate loans to 10%, the person who buys hard-money mortgages cannot make more than that 10%. (In a few cases he makes more from prepayment penalties, and, if he handles his own collections, from late charges.) If the home mortgage company handles the collections, they usually take the late charges as a legitimate payment for their loan service expenses.) But I can buy a mortgage with a set rate as low as 6% and convert it to a yield of 12 or 14 or 16% if the discount, loan life, and installment payment are all favorable.

● I LIKE THE DISCOUNTING OPERATION

Here is my second reason. Given the same rate of return, I would still prefer the discounting operation. It allows me to deal with people during the investigation period, during the negotiation for the purchase, and throughout the life of the loan as I collect the payments. I find a certain satisfaction in those personal relationships.

A third reason follows from the fact that I have been in the discounting business for some time, which means that my bookkeeping system is set up to handle my affairs on that basis.

● PRIDE OF OWNERSHIP

There is a fourth reason for my attitude, a personal opinion that is not based on any records or statistics and may not be valid. But I think that there are more collection problems with hard-money mortgages than with purchase-money mortgages. A new owner, signing that second mortgage to enable him to own his first home, is more enthusiastic and full of pride. You will find him hard at work planting, altering, and improving. You can be sure he doesn't want to lose that new home. He makes his payments. Later, when his improved home becomes more valuable, a new influence enters the picture. He now has a substantial equity he doesn't want to lose. The payments continue.

● BUDGET PROBLEMS

I consider the possibility that a hard-money mortgage may suggest collection problems—problems that outweigh the fact that the security of the property may be excellent. I ask myself this question, "Assuming this to be an emergency for the homeowner, how does it happen that he could not manage his budget in such a way as to provide a cushion for such an emergency?" The corollary to that question is this, "If he had trouble with his budget before he signed up for this second mortgage, how will he manage with an additional monthly installment to be paid?"

There is another thought that nags at me. I wonder if the home-owner is really trying to sell his property piecemeal, borrowing on his equity as fast as it is generated. If he is doing that, then I am not loaning money; I am buying his house. I am not interested in buying houses because I am in the mortgage investment business, not the real estate business.

Perhaps these questions arouse an anxiety that is not warranted. Homeowners who borrow money on hard-money second mort-gages do manage to make their payments; very few would ever consider the disposal of their homes by the foreclosure route.

However, this personal attitude toward the credit problems of these borrowers does fortify my primary reasons. I seldom buy hard-money second mortgages.

● SOME HARD-MONEY SECOND MORTGAGES ARE GOOD INVESTMENTS

In conclusion, I must say that I do not advise others to avoid hard-money second mortgages. The interest rate is satisfactory, and I can think of three cases where such a purchase should definitely appeal to an investor.

The first, as mentioned earlier, is when the lender is too busy with his own business affairs. I would tell him to take the time, in the beginning, to determine that he is working with a depend-able home mortgage company—and then continue—earning his 10% while delegating a great part of the operation to that company.

A second case is one where the homeowner needs a new second mortgage to cover the final balloon payment on a purchase-money mortgage that was set up for a time period that was too short. The lender may be continuing to assist a conscientious buyer, still proud of his home investment, who could only complete his orig-inal, required down payment on the installment plan.

The third case in which any lender would consider financing a hard-money second mortgage is one where the lender himself is a renter and would be delighted to secure the house for his own use. Such a lender could start foreclosure proceedings after a very short period of default. To his surprise, he might not get the house, because hard-pressed owners sometimes accomplish miracles of digging up money that wasn't there. After his failure to acquire the property, however, he would be pleased to find that he has im-pressed upon one homeowner the importance of punctuality.

● LOAN BROKERS

In many eastern states the investor who wants to put his money into hard-money second mortgages would seek a loan broker, one who specializes in small real estate loans to homeowners. Sometimes these brokers arrange small and medium-sized first mortgages. In general, however, they will be arranging second mortgages in almost exactly the same way that home mortgage firms promote these loans in California.

In many states, these loans will be at a different rate of interest than the 10% maximum permitted in California. In several states, the rate of interest will be 12%; in a few states, it will be higher.

12

KEEP AN EYE
ON THOSE SECONDS

● SECOND MORTGAGES WERE
A GAMBLE

Before an investor makes an all-out commitment to the high returns of second mortgages, whether they be discounted purchase-money or fresh hard-money, it would be wise to consider their recent history. Seventy years ago, there were not many second mortgages. As a matter of fact, there were not so many first mortgages either. Ordinary city people rented their houses from landlords who owned extensive property outright. When there was a mortgage on the landlord's property, it was conservative, based on a loan at a figure far below the market value of the real estate.

As our standard of living improved, more and more middle-class citizens were able to move over into the propertied class. They were aided by the extension of amortized loans, the growth of specialized real estate financing institutions, and the increase of funds available for home loans. During this period, the investing class learned that there were many advantages to a more general home ownership. A homeowner took better care of the property than a renter; the investor was relieved of the cost of real estate taxes and repairs; monthly installments were easier to collect than rental payments.

Then came the New Deal, with unemployment insurance, pensions, welfare programs, and other measures that put a financial floor under the entire population. Anyone could save up the money for a down payment and buy his own home. Aided by a constant movement toward lower down payments, federal guarantees of home loans, and favorable treatment of installment payments in their income tax returns, millions of people became homeowners.

In the beginning, this wider, deferred-payment home ownership was limited by a reasonably substantial down payment and a restricted maturity date on the first mortgage. These large down payments meant that there were only a limited number of second mortgages, which were considered to be the wildest kind of speculative gamble. The survival of this point of view among older investors can be gauged by such remarks, still heard, as, "I would never buy a second mortgage under any circumstances," or "I might consider a second mortgage if the discount were 90%."

● SECOND MORTGAGES BECAME RESPECTABLE

However, prosperity and economic stability persisted and extended to more and more people. A few builders and homeowners, eager to sell their houses, began to transfer them to new owners on the basis of low down payments and high-interest second mortgages. Sometimes the sellers kept these seconds; sometimes they sold them at high discounts. A few hardy investors bought these second mortgages, gambling on long shots to get the high interest and the discount pay-back profits. After World War II, principally in California, Texas, and Florida, where real estate values were rising at fantastic rates, investors discovered that second mortgages were quite safe.

Let me demonstrate this new-found safety by a specific case. In 1939, when I was shopping for a house, I was offered a new two-bedroom home in Burbank, a suburb of Los Angeles, for $4,200. The proposed financing was to be a $700 down payment, a $3,000 first mortgage, and a $500 second mortgage. Although I didn't buy this house, I know how its value has increased. So I can show you how that second mortgage investment acquired almost unlimited protection. In eight years, this house was worth $10,000. In 1955, its market price was about $15,000. Today it would sell for more than $20,000. I don't know whether the payments were kept up on that $500 second mortgage. But, as you can see, that is not important. If the investor in that second mortgage had to foreclose, he obtained a property which, if held to the present, would have turned his $500 into $17,000.

This situation was duplicated again and again, in the cities of California, Arizona, Texas, and all the other places where real estate values were rising. Second mortgages in these areas became respectable and safe. They were used to promote the sale of new tracts and old houses. They were used to provide the homeowner with money to buy his second car and his television set. They became a legitimate part of the economy. And they spread to every corner of the United States.

This history is a happy record for both the homeowner and the second mortgage investor. But this favorable record stemmed from factors which should be given some attention. Those factors were prosperity, rising real estate values, and inflation, three things that worked to insure the profit and security of the second mortgage investor. If those tendencies continue to operate, all is well. Happy days are here to stay.

● WHEN SKIES DARKEN

But we must consider the other side of the picture, for we are investing our money in long-range loans with no opportunity to go to the teller's window and withdraw our funds in cash. We must ask ourselves about the effect of recession, deflation, and stationary real estate values.

In one area, the situation might not be as bad as one might think. This bright spot can be found when we consider the often-quoted remark, "People have to live someplace." Our homeowners must continue to pay for the roof over their heads. Many of them will tighten their belts and come through in good shape. We should also consider the established welfare systems that will aid that homeowner whom we have chosen on the basis of his credit and good faith. From somewhere—unemployment checks, pension payments, welfare allowances—those monthly payments will materialize.

● DEPRECIATION

The real danger is to the security behind the mortgage. In a deflationary situation, property values will not only stop rising—they will drop. In either case, an old-fashioned villain will promptly appear, ready to demolish the security. His name is depreciation.

During the last 30 years few people considered depreciation, because the price of a house and lot went up much faster than the structural portion of the property could wear out. If land values stop going up, however, wear and tear on the house must be considered. Depreciation will operate to reduce the value of the security, which consists of both land and improvements on the land.

Let me make this clearer with an example. You buy a $4,000 second mortgage on a new $25,000 house which has an $18,000 first mortgage. (You can calculate the down payment at $3,000.) Since the house was sold by a builder, there is his profit to consider. Although the market price was $25,000, the cost price was probably nearer $21,500. Right after your purchase of that mortgage, we enter a tight real estate market in a deflationary economy. The market value of the house slips a bit, and the homeowner's four children help the process of wear and tear. In two years, the house looks like it's ten years old. The homeowner defaults and you foreclose.

After paying $1,000 in foreclosure costs, you have a house with a $17,500 first mortgage. If you can find buyers for it, how much do you think they will pay?—$21,000, $20,000, $19,500? I suggest that you get out your pencil, allow $500 for repairs, $1,400 for sales costs, and then try to figure how much money you stand to lose on this deal.

● IT COULD NEVER BE THIS BAD

While we are looking at the dark side of the picture, let's consider the risks of an investor's overconcentration on second mortgages, which could be dangerous in any kind of an economic situation. But let us make this look as bad as possible. Let's dream up the worst possible nightmare.

Mr. Norton buys six second mortgages. One by one, the homeowners become delinquent. Two years later, he finds that he has taken over four of them and is in the process of foreclosing on the other two. Since the first mortgage payments range from $75 to $160, he finds that he is paying out $750 a month on six houses and not one cent is coming in from his erstwhile second mortgages. He is also paying hundreds of dollars in foreclosure fees, taxes, and repair bills. He is, quite succinctly, sunk.

● IS THE HOMEOWNER KEEPING UP
THE PAYMENTS ON THE FIRST MORTGAGE?

There is another added danger to your investment in second mortgages. Sometimes the homeowner pays your small payments but fails to make his payments on the first mortgage. The first mortgagee notifies you that the homeowner is in default, and they are about to foreclose on their mortgage. If you do nothing, the first mortgagee will have the property put up for sale and your lien on the property will be "wiped out," as you will have no claim on the new owner.

If you want to protect your interest, you must make all the defaulted first mortgage payments plus late charges at once (or within the redemption period) and you must notify the homeowner that he must reimburse you for this advance. If he fails to take care of this obligation at once, you proceed to foreclose. Your foreclosure action is now based on his default in repaying your advance to the first mortgagee instead of a failure to make the second mortgage payments. But the costs, to you, are the same as those outlined above—plus the two or three months of back first mortgage payments that you have just paid.

The same situation arises when the homeowner fails to pay his taxes or his fire insurance premium. You must be prepared to pay these items, make a demand for immediate payment by the homeowner, and, if he fails to arrange for payment, proceed to foreclose.

Because of the added risks and possible expenses involved in second mortgages, many conservative mortgage discounters will not restrict themselves to these mortgages. Their policy is to buy several conservative mortgages—good firsts or very well-seasoned seconds—for every high-discount second mortgage they purchase.

● I MOVED UP TO FIRST MORTGAGES

For my part, I have followed a planned policy (during the last few years) of moving up to first mortgages. As you can imagine, it isn't easy. You may have four or five second mortgages that pay between $20 and $40 a month each. Your total cash receipts are only a little more than $100 a month. At that rate, it takes a year to generate enough for another small second mortgage. So you are in no position to go into the market for a $10,000 first mortgage. But I have done it—and I advise you to strain every resource to follow in my footsteps.

My first step, after acquiring seven or eight second mortgages, was to be very hesitant about investing in additional seconds, no matter how good they appeared to be. I was waiting for a small first mortgage. One did come along—the $1,300 mortgage with the $65 payments that I mentioned in the chapter on seasoning. This was a big step forward, because it significantly increased my monthly cash flow. I continued my cautious approach, banking my money and making several small investments in blue chip stocks. Luckily, one of these stocks produced a quick capital gain of $900. Another small first mortgage, with a balance of $1,700, came on the market at a low discount. I grabbed it and saw my monthly cash flow increase by another $75.

By this time, I was convinced that I could make the move from second mortgages to firsts. The Rivera mortgage, which required a $10,000 investment, was a considerable strain, but I managed it. I had to borrow from my bank and I had to sell my remaining corporate bonds (which were dropping in value anyway). The Rivera deal added another $80 to my monthly cash flow and helped pay off the bank loan. A year later, from the sale of 100 shares of a good stock and a very small bank loan, I was able to purchase a $6,200 first mortgage at a 10% discount which added another $75 monthly installment.

With that purchase, I graduated. I can now buy either first or second mortgages, according to my judgment as to their safety and profit. In the past year and a half, I have made the following purchases: An extremely well-seasoned $750 second mortgage at a 22% discount, a new $2,800 second at a 37% discount, a seasoned $1,300 first at a 15% discount, a $4,600 first at a 20% discount, and a $6,000 first at a 20% discount. As you can see, the ratio runs 3:2 in favor of firsts by number and more than 3:1 in favor of firsts by total investment. The higher cash flow from first mortgages is worth emphasizing, too, as it puts me in position to continue a more selective attitude. (Incidentally, my list of purchases does not mean I had a $12,000 cash flow for the period. I had the cooperation of my banker.)

13

A CHECKLIST
FOR YOUR DOCUMENTS

● THE MORTGAGE PURCHASE
TRANSACTION

I have given many examples of mortgage purchases without presenting an exact account of the transfer process. This oversight was deliberate—a planned omission which was necessary to keep us from getting bogged down in legal matters during our general discussion of mortgage investment. It is now time to correct this intentional oversight by providing a descriptive list of the documents required, so that you can be fully protected from the time you part with your money until the last installment is paid.

As an introduction to this chapter, as well as an assurance that a layman does know something about a subject that is the province of legal experts on real estate, I will tell you how I gained a working knowledge of these matters.

I told you that I started out by buying a $12,400 first mortgage and a $2,400 second mortgage. I had given Gardner a check to hold the first deal when I was in his office between the two trips to look at the houses. At that time, we had arranged for a meeting on the following afternoon to tie up the deal for the first mortgage. But I was in touch with Gardner before that. When I got home after looking at the smaller house, I called him to tell him that I wanted the second mortgage also. Gardner was willing to hold the other mortgage for me without an additional deposit; we could handle the purchase arrangements for both deals at the same time.

The moment I finished that telephone call, I began to worry. It wasn't that I was concerned about the quality of the two mortgages. I was fearful of being in the clutches of two strangers—the broker, Gardner, and the lawyer who operated the escrow office. They knew all about real estate, while I knew absolutely nothing. I finally called an attorney and told him my problem. I proposed to pay whatever fee was necessary to get legal advice that would get me safely through the transactions slated for the following afternoon. The attorney told me to come to his office the next morning to get written instructions that would tell me exactly how to proceed.

● I PAID FOR LEGAL ADVICE

When I walked into the attorney's office the next day, he handed me a single typewritten sheet with a numbered list of documents. I read that list and shook my head. "I have no idea what any of this means," I confessed.

"You don't have to know what they mean, nor do you need a complete legal explanation." The attorney tapped the paper with his finger. "Just read off this list and tell the broker and the escrow officer that you will not make your deal unless they take care of every item. I can assure you that they will both understand exactly what is required."

"Is all this customary?" I asked.

"The complete list is for the legally correct purchase of a second mortgage," the lawyer said. Then he leaned forward and checked off two items. "You won't need these two in your escrow contract for the first mortgage."

"All right," I said, "since I'm paying for this list I'd better use it."

As I wrote out the check for the fee my attorney quipped, "The next time you come in here to pay my fees, I'll charge you a great deal more. By that time you'll have mortgages all over town."

When I read off my lawyer's list at the escrow office, Gardner frowned in annoyance. The escrow man, however, complimented me for helping out with the preparation of a proper set of escrow instructions. He then explained the importance of the items as he wrote them into the escrow form, a process that helped me gain a better understanding of what we were doing. As soon as the escrow instructions were typed, the broker ran through them and remarked, "I haven't seen such a precise list of requirements in years."

"That's because you have slipped into an informal manner of transferring mortgages," said the escrow officer.

"I guess you're right," said Gardner. He signed the two forms.

I checked the escrow instructions against my list. Then my wife and I signed them. Later, when all the documents were sent to me, I was able to study them and work out the reason for the importance of each one.

Instead of giving you the list my lawyer gave me, I will take up the items, one by one, and provide a simple and complete explanation about each one.

● THE PROMISSORY NOTE

The first paper you must have is the original promissory note. This is just what its name says, a signed promise to pay. Any promissory note may be used in a mortgage transaction, but it is generally an installment-type note which refers to the mortgage of the same date that secures the note. It is signed by the homeowner (and wife) and promises to pay the total indebtedness at a certain rate of interest, with payments to be made at specified times. It states, "Each payment shall be credited first on interest then due and the remainder on principal; and interest shall thereupon cease on the principal so credited." It may require payment of the balance due at a certain time or it may state that the payments will continue until all principal and interest have been paid. This note must be endorsed over to you by the previous mortgagee. The endorsement will be on the back of the note, written in the same manner that an endorsement is written on a check. If there is no place for the endorsement on the back, it will be on a separate piece of paper attached to the note. The signature on this endorsement must be identical to the name of the person to whom the note was made out. If the note was made out to two or more persons, the endorsement must be signed by all of those parties. (See page 94.)

INSTALLMENT NOTE

SECURED BY DEED OF TRUST

DO NOT DESTROY THIS NOTE. When paid this note, with Deed of Trust securing same, must be surrendered to Trustee.

$ <u>10,000.00</u>   Los Angeles, California. <u>June 10</u> , 19<u>67</u>

FOR VALUE RECEIVED, the undersigned promise (~~s~~) to pay <u>Fred Jones and Mary Jones, husband and wife</u> , or order at <u>Los Angeles, California</u> the sum of <u>Ten thousand and no/100</u> Dollars, with interest from <u>June 10</u> , 19 <u>67</u> on unpaid principal at the rate of <u>7</u> per cent per annum; principal and interest payable in installments of <u>Ninety and no/100</u> Dollars <u>or more</u> on the <u>10th</u> day of each month beginning on the <u>10th</u> day of <u>July</u> , 19 <u>67</u> and continuing until all interest and principal have been paid.

Each payment shall be credited first on interest then due and the remainder on principal; and interest shall thereupon cease on the principal so credited. If default be made in payment of any installment when due, the whole sum of principal and interest shall become immediately due at the option of the holder of this note. Principal and interest are payable in lawful money of the United States. If action be instituted on this note, the undersigned promise (~~s~~) to pay such sum as the Court may fix as attorney's fees.

This note is secured by a Deed of Trust to <u>Titanic</u> <u>Escrow Corporation</u> as Trustee, on real estate located in <u>Los Angeles</u> County, California.

<u>John Homeowner</u>

<u>Mary Homeowner</u>

Specimen document prepared by author. Names and terms are fictitious.

Figure 13-1. *Sample promissory note used with a trust deed (mortgage).*

● THE MORTGAGE

The second paper is the original mortgage (or trust deed). This is a printed document with spaces which have been filled in with the name of the mortgagee, a legal description of the property, and the total of the debt in a paragraph referring to a certain note "of even date." It will have the signatures (notarized) of the home-owners, which you must check, to insure that they are identical to the signatures on the note.

On the back of many mortgages, you will find paragraph after paragraph of fine print which outline the precise obligations of the borrower and lender (mortgagor and mortgagee). In some states, however, the detailed mortgage terms are not included in the actual document. Instead, there is a paragraph which reads that both borrower and lender agree to all the terms and provisions of a certain "sample mortgage," and specifies where that "sample mortgage" is recorded. (See pages 96-99.)

● THE ASSIGNMENT

The third paper is an assignment of the mortgage. This is a printed document with a space for your name and a space for the legal description of the property. See that your name (or your own and your spouse's name) is correctly written. You must check to be sure that the inserted legal description is identical to that on the original mortgage. (A variation of this description of the property is to refer to the legal description in the original mortgage and to identify that original mortgage as a specific document by number, page, and book of its official recording.) This assignment will be signed by the person who is selling you the mortgage. That signature must be the same as the name of the mortgagee on the original mortgage and identical to the signature on the endorsement of the note. This document must be recorded.

Sometimes the mortgage has passed through several hands. In that case, you must check the several endorsements that are attached to the original promissory note. There will be a series of assignments, which you should follow through, step by step, checking legal descriptions and signatures. The original mortgage comes to you just as it was made out and signed. (See page 100.)

● TITLE INSURANCE

The fourth document you must get is a policy of title insurance (or abstract of title). This will consist of a folder of several papers.

REAL ESTATE MORTGAGE
SHORT FORM

This Indenture, Made the _____ day of _____, 19____

By _____
_____, hereinafter designated as Mortgagor,

To _____
_____, hereinafter designated as Mortgagee,

Witnesseth: That the Mortgagor mortgages to the said Mortgagee the real property situate in the
County of _____, State of California, and described as follows, to-wit:

Together with all and singular the tenements, hereditaments and appurtenances thereunto belonging, or in
anywise appertaining, and the reversion or reversions, remainder and remainders, rents, issues and profits
thereof.

As Security for the payment of _____ true cop_____, to-wit:

following _____ Promissory Note_____, of which the

Courtesy of Wolcotts, Inc., a subsidiary of American Stationery Products Corp.

Figure 13-2. *A standard mortgage form.*

$ _____

_____ after date, for value received, _____ promise to pay to

_____ , 19 ___

or order, at _____ , the sum of

_____ Dollars,

with interest at the rate of _____ per cent per _____ from date, until paid, interest

payable _____ , and if not so paid to be compounded _____

and bear the same rate of interest as the principal; and should the interest not be paid

then the whole sum of principal and interest shall become immediately due and payable at the option of

the holder of this note. Principal and interest payable in lawful money of the United States.

AND THE MORTGAGOR promises to pay said note _____ according to the terms and conditions thereof, and in case of default in the payment of the same, or of any installment of interest thereon when due, the Mortgagee, or _____ assigns, may declare the whole debt immediately due and payable, and may foreclose this mortgage, and may include in such foreclosure a reasonable counsel fee, to be fixed by the Court, together with all payments made by the Mortgagee for taxes and assessments on said premises, including taxes on the interest of the Mortgagee therein by reason of this Mortgage; and for insurance of the buildings on said premises paid by the Mortgagee, and for any adverse claims to the mortgaged property paid by Mortgagee as well as the cost of searching title to the mortgaged premises, subsequent to the execution hereof, all of which payments the Mortgagee is hereby authorized to make, and the same with interest thereon at the same rate as provided in said Promissory Note _____, together with said counsel fees, are secured by this mortgage, and payable to the Mortgagee, or _____ assigns, in United States lawful money, out of the proceeds of sale under said foreclosure.

WITNESS the hand ___ and seal ___ of the Mortgagor.

MORTGAGE—SHORT FORM (NOTE 1442)—WOLCOTTS FORM 1062—REVISED 2-64

8 pt. type or larger

Figure 13-2. *(Contd.)*

THIS SPACE FOR RECORDER'S USE ONLY

STATE OF CALIFORNIA,

} ss.

County of _____

ON _____, 19 ____, before me, the undersigned, a Notary Public in and for said State, personally appeared _____ known to me to be the person ____ whose name ____ subscribed to the within Instrument, and acknowledged to me that ____he ____ executed the same.

WITNESS my hand and official seal.

_____
NAME (TYPED OR PRINTED)
Notary Public in and for said State.

ORDER NO. _____

When recorded, please mail this
Instrument to

_____
_____
_____

Figure 13-2. *(Contd.)*

TOGETHER WITH the rents, issues, royalties and profits thereof, SUBJECT HOWEVER, to the right, power and authority hereinafter given to and conferred upon Beneficiary to collect and apply such rents, issues, royalties and profits.

For the Purpose of Securing

(1.) Performance of each agreement of Trustor contained herein. (2.) Payment of the indebtedness evidenced by one promissory note of even date herewith in the principal sum of $..............executed by Trustor and payable to Beneficiary or order, and extensions or renewals thereof.

A. To protect the security of this Deed of Trust, Trustor agrees:

1. To keep said property in good condition and repair; not to remove or demolish any building thereon; to complete or restore promptly and in good and workmanlike manner any building which may be constructed, damaged or destroyed thereon; to pay when due all claims for labor performed and materials furnished therefor; to comply with all laws affecting said property or requiring any alterations or improvements to be made thereon; not to commit or permit waste thereof; not to commit, suffer or permit any act upon said property in violation of law; to cultivate, irrigate, fertilize, fumigate, prune and do all other acts which from the character or use of said property may be reasonably necessary, the specific enumerations herein not excluding the general.

2. To provide, maintain and deliver to Beneficiary fire insurance satisfactory to and with loss payable to Beneficiary. The amount collected under any fire or other insurance policy may be applied by Beneficiary upon any indebtedness secured hereby and in such order as Beneficiary may determine, or at option of Beneficiary the entire amount so collected or any part thereof may be released to Trustor. Such application or release shall not cure or waive any default or notice of default hereunder or invalidate any act done pursuant to such notice.

3. To appear in and defend any action or proceeding purporting to affect the security hereof or the rights or powers of Beneficiary or Trustee; and to pay all costs and expenses, including cost of evidence of title and attorney's fees in a reasonable sum, in any such action or proceeding in which Beneficiary or Trustee may appear, or in any action or proceeding instituted by Beneficiary or Trustee to protect or enforce the security of this Deed of Trust or the obligations secured hereby.

4. To pay: at least ten days before delinquency all taxes and assessments affecting said property, including assessments on appurtenant water stock; when due, all incumbrances, charges and liens, with interest, on said property or any part thereof, which appear to be prior or superior hereto; all costs, fees and expenses of this Trust.

5. Should Trustor fail to make any payment or to do any act as in this Subdivision A hereof provided, then Beneficiary or Trustee, but without obligation so to do and without notice to or demand upon Trustor and without releasing Trustor from any obligation hereof, may: make or do the same in such manner and to such extent as either may deem necessary to protect the security hereof, Beneficiary or Trustee being authorized to enter upon said property for such purposes; appear in and defend any action or proceeding purporting to affect the security hereof or the rights or powers of Beneficiary or Trustee; pay, purchase, contest or compromise any incumbrance, charge or lien which in the judgment of either appears to be prior or superior hereto; and, in exercising any such powers, pay necessary expenses, employ counsel and pay his reasonable fees.

6. To pay immediately and without demand all sums so expended by Beneficiary or Trustee, with interest from date of expenditure at the rate called for in the note secured hereby, or at seven per cent per annum, whichever is greater, and the repayment thereof shall be secured hereby.

Figure 13-3. *The fine print at the bottom of a trust deed (mortgage).*

WHEN RECORDED MAIL TO · D. Robert Burleigh	SPACE FOR RECORDER'S USE
2518 Rinconia Dr. Los Angeles, Calif. 90068	ASSIGNMENT OF DEED OF TRUST

FOR VALUE RECEIVED, the undersigned hereby grants, assigns and transfers to D. Robert Burleigh and Fern S. Burleigh, husband and wife, as joint tenants all beneficial interest to a Deed of Trust dated March 23, 19 68, executed by John Homeowner and Mary Homeowner, husband and wife, Trustor(s), to Titanic Escrow Corporation, Trustee, and recorded as Instrument No. 4321 on April 3, 19 68, in Book T3366, Page 789, of Official Records in the office of the County Recorder of Los Angeles County, California,

TOGETHER with the note or notes therein referred to, the money due, including interest, and all rights under said Deed of Trust.

Date: August 15, 19 68

Fred Jones

Elizabeth Jones

STATE OF CALIFORNIA
COUNTY OF Los Angeles } SS.

On August 15, 1968
before me, the undersigned
Notary Public in said State,
personally appeared
Fred Jones
Elizabeth Jones

(SEAL)

known to me to be the person (s)
whose name (s) appear on this
instrument and acknowledged
that they executed the same.

WITNESS my hand and Official Seal

Frank Notary

Specimen document prepared by author. Names and terms are fictitious.

Figure 13-4. *Assignment of a trust deed (mortgage).*

Policy # AR 873 - 0722

TITANIC TITLE, LTD.
hereinafter called the Company,

GUARANTEES the parties listed in Schedule A, their heirs and successors, against loss by reason of any incorrectness of land title (hereinafter described) except items noted in Exceptions, Schedule A, and those liens and encumbrances listed in Parts 1 and 2, Schedule B. This Guaranty is limited to actual loss sustained by the named insured parties, as set forth in Section II; and in no case shall the Company be obligated for an amount exceeding the Liability stated in Schedule A, together with legal expenses and attorney fees which may become obligations of the Company to protect the validity of title as stipulated in Section II.

SCHEDULE A

LIABILITY: $12,000.00   FEE: $58.00

INSURED

John Homeowner and Mary Homeowner,
Fred Jones and Elizabeth Jones, mortgagees.

DESCRIPTION OF PROPERTY

Lot 152, Block 123, Tract 1776, in the City of Los Angeles, as per map recorded in Book 431, Page 210, in the office of the County Recorder, County of Los Angeles, State of California.

EFFECTIVE DATE: July 21, 1967

EXCEPTIONS

Personal debts or claims against John Homeowner and Mary Homeowner.

Specimen document prepared by author. Names and terms are fictitious.

Figure 13-5. *Title insurance policy in simplified guaranty form.*

For Bank Use Only: Prepare In Triplicate.

OFFSET STATEMENT

SUMMERDALE FIRST NATIONAL BANK

Outpost _____ BRANCH

Culver City, _____ CALIFORNIA

DATE July 1, 1967

ESCROW NO. CC 4315

Mr. and Mrs. John Homeowner
8932 E. Ridge Road
Culver City, California

An escrow has been opened at this Branch by Fred Jones and Elizabeth Jones covering an assignment of a note secured by a TRUST DEED recorded on June 18 , 19 66 , in Book T1234 Document/File/Page No. 111 , of Official Records of Los Angeles County, California, covering Lot 152 , Block 123 , Tract 1776 in the City of Culver City,

of said County, which real property we are informed is owned by you.

The note secured by said Trust Deed is in the original amount of $12,000.00 dated June 10 , 19 66 , executed by John Homeowner and Mary Homeowner of Fred Jones and Elizabeth Jones

Please fill in and sign the original of the **Owner's Offset Statement** below and return the entire page. RETAIN COPY FOR YOUR RECORDS.

Figure 13-6. *Owner's offset statement (specimen.)*

SUMMERDALE FIRST NATIONAL BANK

By _____ Mildred Mack

(DO NOT DETACH)

OWNER'S OFFSET STATEMENT

Escrow No. CC 4315

Date July 1, 1967

Summerdale First National Bank

I hereby certify that I am the owner of the real property encumbered by the TRUST DEED described above.

That no advances, other than the original Principal, have been made, EXCEPT $ _____

That the unpaid balance of the Principal of said Note plus advances, if any, is $ 11,732.50

That the interest on said Note at the rate of ____% per annum has been paid to June 1, 1967

That no change in the original terms of said note and encumbrance has been made, except _____

That the total funds now held by the holder of said note for future payments of Fire Insurance, Taxes and Assessments, and Mortgage Insurance is $ _____ Last monthly payment including impounds was $ _____

That the makers of said Note received full and valid consideration therefor, and said encumbrance and Note are valid. That no part of the Principal or Interest of said Note has been paid, EXCEPT as herein stated. That I have no offsets, claims or defenses against said Note, except as herein stated. I understand that the said Note is being assigned and I make this statement for your benefit and that of all parties in interest, including assignee in said note, and understand that it is being relied upon by all of said parties.

Street Address _____

City & Zip Code _____

(Telephone)

Signature _____

Signature _____

Figure 13-6. *(Contd.)*

10725

HOME OWNERS CHANGE ENDORSEMENT

CHANGE ENDORSEMENT

TRANSURANCE For HOME OWNERS

Property and Casualty Insurer from Transamerica Corporation

From **Premier Insurance Company**

POLICY NUMBER
XAC-12345

Check all areas of change and provide change information.
Complete additional sections as required.

| AGENT'S CODE | AGENT'S NAME |
| YA | Charles Insbroker |

EFFECTIVE DATE
Month 8 Day 22 Year 1968

BILL CONTINUOUS PREMIUMS TO:
☒ Insured ☐ Mortgagee ☐ Servicing Agency

ADDITIONAL INSURED NAME AND ADDRESS

NAME OF INSURED (If change of insured complete No. 2 below)
John Homeowner and Mary Homeowner

House Number and Street (If change of home complete No. 1 below)
3214 W. Main St.

LOAN NUMBER
B - 38

DESCRIBE INTEREST
First mortgagees

City Los Angeles, California   State   Zip Code 90005

LOCATION OF PREMISES IF OTHER THAN MAILING ADDRESS
Same

MORTGAGE OR SERVICE AGENCY
D. Robert Burleigh and Fern S. Burleigh, husband and wife, as joint tenants

TYPE OF POLICY
☐ Standard   ☐ Special   ☐ Tenants

LOSS DEDUCTIBLE APPLICABLE – SECTION I.

$_____ To loss to all covered property from all perils except wind and hail damage to dwelling and appurtenant structures.

$_____ To loss to dwelling and appurtenant structures from windstorm and hail.

COVERAGES: The limits of liability are amended as follows:

| Section Chg | Limits of Liability | Basic Coverages |

The description of the described premises shown on the declarations page is deleted and the following description is substituted therefor:

CONSTRUCTION
☐ Frame (Not otherwise classified)
☐ Frame with Aluminum

TYPE OF DWELLING
☐ Residential ☐ Secondary
☐ Apartment ☐ Other (Specify)
☐ Town House
☐ Condominium

Zone	Protection		Premium
	Class		Group
	Not more than		Not more than

I

A. Described Dwelling $20,000.00
B. Appurtenant Private Structures $_____.00
C. Unscheduled Personal Property $_____.00
D. Additional Living Expense $_____.00

II

E. Personal Liability $_____000.00
F. Medical Payments to Others $_____.00 (Each Person)
$25,000.00 Each Occurrence

Courtesy of Transamerica Insurance Group.

Figure 13-7. *Fire insurance endorsement.*

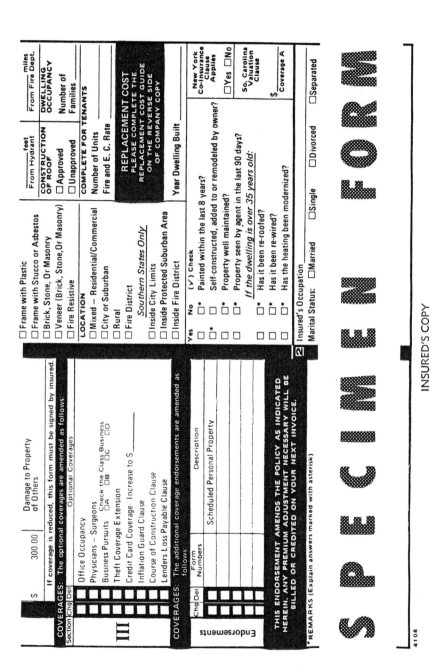

Figure 13-7. *(Contd.)*

It will contain the amount of insurance coverage on the validity of title, which must be as much as the balance owing on the mortgage. It will give you a legal description of the property, a list of easements, status of mineral and water rights, list of liens against the property, and the status of taxes. Again, you must see that your name is correct, that the legal description agrees with that on the original mortgage, and you must be sure that there are no liens prior to your own mortgage (except for senior mortgages of which you had been told). Your own mortgage will be listed twice, as the recorded instrument of the original and as a notation that it has been assigned to you. You should make sure that there are no delinquent taxes. (See page 101.)

● THE OWNER'S OFFSET STATEMENT

The fifth paper is an owner's offset statement (sometimes called an estoppel agreement). This statement—showing the balance due on the note, the amount of the regular monthly payments, the rate of interest, and the date to which interest has been paid—bears the homeowner's signature. The importance of this signed statement is obvious. You don't want to get into a situation where you are trying to collect a specified debt under specified conditions which the homeowner claims to be incorrect. Once you get a confirmation from the homeowner, during the transfer period, there can be no argument about the amount still due. (See pages 102-103.)

● THE FIRE INSURANCE POLICY

The sixth paper is generally a delayed document. You want your name listed as mortgagee on the fire (or householder) insurance policy in place of the former mortgagee. It may be handled during the escrow period by an insurance endorsement, or it would be satisfactory if the former mortgagee wrote a letter (with a copy to you) to the insurance carrier requesting that your name replace his as mortgagee. Once your name is on that insurance policy, the insurance company will never settle a damage claim without including you in the settlement. (See pages 104-105.)

You now have the six documents that insure a legal transfer of a first mortgage to you.

For the transfer of a second mortgage, you need these six and two additional documents.

WHEN RECORDED MAIL TO	
D. Robert Burleigh	**SPACE FOR RECORDER'S USE**
2518 Rinconia Dr.	
Los Angeles, Calif.	**REQUEST FOR NOTICE**
90068	

Pursuant to Section 2924B of the California Civil Code, request is made that copies of any Default Notice and Notice of Sale affecting a Deed of Trust recorded ___July 22___, 19 65 as Instrument No.___12345___ in Book___T8421___, Page 400, Official Records of___Los Angeles___ County, California executed by ___John Homeowner and Mary Homeowner,___ husband and wife, _____, trustor (s), in which ___Titanic Savings and Loan Association___ is designated as beneficiary, and ___Titanic Escrow Corporation___ is designated as trustee,

be mailed to___D. Robert Burleigh___
whose address is ___2518 Rinconia Drive___
___Los Angeles, California   90068___

STATE OF CALIFORNIA ⎫ SS.
COUNTY of Los Angeles ⎭

On___August 15, 1966___
before me, the undersigned Notary Public in said State, personally appeared

___Fred Jones___

___Elizabeth Jones___

Fred Jones

Elizabeth Jones

(SEAL)

_____
known to me to be the person (s) whose name (s) appear on this instrument and acknowledged that ___they___ executed the same.

WITNESS my hand and Official Seal

Frank Notary

Specimen document prepared by author. Names and terms are fictitious.

Figure 13-8. *Request for notice form.*

CITIZENS
savings and loan association

814 STATE STREET • SANTA BARBARA, CALIFORNIA
WOODLAND 6-1551

Date: __February 26, 1962__

Your Escrow No.: __2744__

Our Loan No.: __LA-8401__

Borrower: _____

Address of Property: __Los Angeles, California__

Golden Bear Escrow Company
3859 W. 6th Street
Los Angeles 5, California

Gentlemen:

Pursuant to your request the following is a statement in regard to the above captioned loan:

Original Amount: $ __3,500.00__   Date of Note: __June 13, 1956__

Monthly Inst.: Principal and Interest $ __35.00__   Taxes $ __-0-__   Total $ __35.00__

Interest: Rate __6__ % Paid to: __February 15, 1962__

Arrearages:

Date Due	Principal & Interest	Tax Fund	Advances	Total
	$	$	$	$
	$	$	$	$

Next Installment Due: __March 15, 1962__

Principal Balance · · · · · $ __2,077.95__   Impounded Funds for Taxes · · · · $ __-0-__

Note contains prepayment penalty as follows: _____

*Courtesy of Golden Bear Escrow Co., Los Angeles, California
and Citizens Savings and Loan Assoc., Santa Barbara, California*

Figure 13-9. *First mortgagee's statement.*

If paid in full on or before _____ $ _____ If paid in full on or before _____ $ _____

(This statement subject to collection of any draft conditionally credited to loan pending payment and actual receipt of funds by Association)

Fire Insurance: _____ Firemen's Insurance Company policy No. CD 13292 in the amount of $8,000.00, expiring June 27, 1962.

As a CONDITION PRECEDENT to the use in any manner of the information contained herein, you are required:

1. To have written authority from above borrower to request this information.

2. To furnish us with a copy of the policy of title insurance issued to new owners of the property.

3. To collect for and remit to this Association all payments and advances due on this loan EXISTING AT THE TIME OF THE CLOSING OF THIS ESCROW.

4. To provide evidence to us that all taxes and assessments against said property that are due and payable have been paid, including taxes that are due: **April 10, 1962**

5. To obtain for delivery to this Association fire insurance conforming to the standards required by this Association in name of new owner(s) with extended coverage and beneficiary's endorsements in favor of this Association and evidence of payment of premiums thereon in the amount of not less than $2,100.00. Average clauses are not acceptable unless expressly approved in writing by the Association.

6. To collect for this Association a transfer fee of $ _____ 10.00

7. That you notify us immediately if within 30 days this escrow is cancelled or not completed.

8. That you obtain signatures of purchaser(s) to enclosed membership proxy.

This Association is not to be put to any expense whatever in connection herewith.
Please sign and return the enclosed copy of these instructions.

Yours very truly,

CITIZENS SAVINGS & LOAN ASSOCIATION

B. A. Burkard
Assistant Secretary

2M 8-59 C.L.C. 134

Figure 13-9. *(Contd.)*

● REQUEST FOR NOTICE

The most important is a form known as a request for notice. This is a short paper, sometimes incorporated with the mortgage assignment, signed by the former mortgagee, which gives your name and address and asks that you be notified if the property is to be sold as the result of foreclosure action by the holder of the first mortgage. This paper must be recorded to be of any value. Although the word "request" seems to be a mild term, this recorded document becomes a powerful protection for you. The holder of the first mortgage cannot ignore you in any action of foreclosure, because his title to the property would not be clear unless he could prove that you were notified prior to his foreclosure sale. (See page 107.)

● THE FIRST MORTGAGEE'S STATEMENT

The second additional document you require for a second mortgage purchase is a first mortgagee's statement (called "an estoppel affidavit" in some states and "a statement of beneficiary" in trust deed states). This is similar to an owner's offset statement mentioned above, except that it gives the same signed information about the date to which interest has been paid and the amount of the principal balance on the first mortgage. It is obtained from the holder of the first mortgage. In the escrow instructions which the seller of the second mortgage has signed, there is a declaration of the approximate balance of the first mortgage. By requiring the first mortgagee's statement, you are guarding against the unexpected discovery that the homeowner's balance on the first mortgage is much greater than you were told. (See pages 108-109.)

The six documents necessary for a first mortgage purchase and the eight required for a safe second mortgage purchase may seem overly legalistic and involved. If you have that feeling, I suggest that you reread Chapter 6 and afterwards go over this chapter a second time. You will then understand the purposes and values of all those papers. After your first purchase of a mortgage and a careful examination of the actual documents (including the fine print), you will accept the entire list as a perfectly normal means of legal protection.

● YOU CAN WAIVE SOME REQUIREMENTS

After you have had some experience in actual transactions, you will find that you need not be quite so strict in demanding every document I have listed and described. Here are the situations: (1) You can often simplify the matter of the title insurance. If the former holder of the mortgage will give you his title insurance policy, you can see that the title was clear up to that date. You can then agree to accept an endorsement of that original title insurance policy, which covers the intervening period and takes care of the really vital point, the title company's guarantee of your security's title up to the amount of the homeowner's indebtedness. (2) In the purchase of either a first or second mortgage, it may be possible to waive the requirement of an owner's offset statement. Such action would be warranted if you and a companion had previously visited the homeowner, seen his payment book, and heard him say that the balance shown therein was correct. You have an *oral* offset statement, witnessed by your friend. (3) In a second mortgage deal you can waive the first mortgagee's statement if, before you buy your mortgage, you can get the loan number of the homeowner's first mortgage and obtain an oral confirmation of the status of that first mortgage. Another case where you could waive that requirement, would be where the seller of a second mortgage has a computer card he has received from the savings and loan company that holds the first mortgage. (In this computer age, many of these companies send this record to the holder of the second mortgage whenever their payment is a few days late.) This card would serve the purpose of the first mortgagee's statement.

● WHEN THE ORIGINAL NOTE AND MORTGAGE ARE MISSING

There are cases where the former mortgagee has lost the original mortgage or the original note, but he wants to sell his rights to collect the homeowner's indebtedness. This does happen occasionally, especially when the former mortgagee has died or become senile.

In the instance where the former mortgagee still has the note but has lost the mortgage, even a beginner can safely buy the note *provided the mortgage was recorded.* You still get the original note, endorsed, and, in place of the original mortgage, you get a photostatic copy of the recorded mortgage, certified. And you have not waived any of the essential documents; you are merely getting the second one, the original mortgage, in a different form.

If the original mortgage has been saved, but the note lost, you have a more complicated problem that will cost money and require legal advice. A beginner should not buy a mortgage where the original promissory note has been lost.

If both mortgage and note have been lost, there is still the pos‑ sibility of purchasing the rights if the mortgage was recorded. A photostatic copy of the mortgage replaces the original and, with legal assistance, it is possible to buy the rights to the lost note.

● NOTIFY THE FIRST MORTGAGEE THAT YOU HOLD THE SECOND MORTGAGE

Before concluding this chapter, I would like to go back for a further discussion of the request for notice. I will repeat here that you must have that document and you must have it recorded. But you should do more—to insure that the critical point of that "notice" does not catch you unawares.

Here is my recommendation. The moment you buy a second mortgage, you should notify the holders of the first mortgage by letter. They will put your name and address in their file and will generally notify you the moment the homeowner is late in making his payments. Secondly, you should get the loan number of the homeowner's first mortgage. In the days before computers, the holder of the second mortgage generally had to write a letter, and often had to pay a fee, to get information on the status of the homeowner's first mortgage. Now, with computer print-outs available in the offices of the savings and loan companies, you can usually get a report of the homeowner's payment status by telephone. You can, therefore, keep yourself informed of the status of payments on the senior obligation.

In spite of these precautions, however, errors are made. You may hear nothing about a default on the first mortgage until the holder of that mortgage actually starts foreclosure. When that happens, your recorded request for notice becomes the essential protection of your security.

● WHO PAYS THE TRANSFER COSTS?

It is general practice for the mortgage seller to pay all the costs of transfer of a discounted purchase-money mortgage; the same thing is true of a hard-money second, for the borrower pays all the fees. But you should not automatically assume that this will always be the case. Have an understanding with the broker and the seller of the mortgage that all costs of escrow, title insurance, broker's fees, recording fees, postage, etc., will be paid by the seller.

SUPERIOR COURT OF THE STATE OF CALIFORNIA
FOR THE COUNTY OF LOS ANGELES

May 8, 1970   Order and Decree No. 84

Dept. 5 of the above entitled Court convened, the Honorable Victor E. Donatelli, Judge Pro Tempore Presiding, and the following proceedings were had:

No. P- 535473

Estate of WILLIAM ENDERS, also known as WILLIAM ROBERT ENDERS, Deceased.

ORDER CONFIRMING SALE OF PERSONAL PROPERTY

Attorney appearing for Petitioner: John D. Maharg, County Counsel.

The return and petition for confirmation of sale of personal property herein of Baldo M. Kristovich, Public Administrator, as administrator of the estate of said deceased, coming on this day for hearing by the Court, all notices of said hearing having been given as required by law, and it appearing to be for the advantage, benefit and best interests of said estate and those interested therein;

It is ordered by the Court that the sale of the personal property hereinafter described, to D. Robert Burleigh and Fern S. Burleigh, husband and wife, as joint tenants, for the sum of $3,678.98, cash, is hereby confirmed; and upon payment of the price aforesaid, said administrator shall execute the necessary instruments of transfer to said purchaser (s) of the personal property described as follows:

Promissory note dated April 24, 1967, executed by E. Wander and Son, a partnership, assumed by Barbara Hubbard, in the principal sum of $5,300.00, secured by deed of trust recorded in Book T5391, Page (s) 960, Official Records of Los Angeles County, California, covering that certain real property described as follows:

The West 30 feet of Lot 43 of Tract No. 4342, in the City of Los Angeles, County of Los Angeles, State of California, as per map recorded in Book 47, Page 25 of Maps, in the office of the County Recorder of said County.

THE DOCUMENT TO WHICH THIS CERTIFICATION IS ATTACHED IS A FULL, TRUE AND CORRECT COPY OF THE ORIGINAL ON FILE AND OF RECORD IN MY OFFICE.

MAY 19 1970 ....19......

ATTEST .... County Clerk and Clerk of the

WILLIAM G. SHARP Superior Court of the State of California in and for the County of Los Angeles

By _____ DEPUTY

Figure 13-10. *Probate order and decree.*

● AN EXTRA DOCUMENT

When you buy a mortgage out of probate, there will be one additional document. It will be supplied by the attorney for the estate and may be one of several legal versions. It is, however, simply an order by the probate judge that directs the executor to sign the assignment in lieu of the former owner (now deceased). (See page 113.)

14

HOW I KEEP BOOKS

● DISCOUNTERS HAVE TO KEEP BOOKS

The ordinary salaried man, with a savings account, a bond or two, and a few shares of stock, can get along with the sketchiest kind of personal bookkeeping. If he operates on a sensible budget, he will make a monthly allocation for annual expenditures like taxes, insurance, etc., and for long-term purchases like furniture, cars, etc. Once he has done this, he can tell from his bank account whether he is operating his personal finances on a sound basis.

The moment you buy your first mortgage, however, you will have to start keeping some simple bookkeeping records. You will need these records for your income taxes, of course, but the real reason for your bookkeeping lies in the threefold character of the monthly installments you will be receiving on your mortgage investments. Part of these monthly pay-

ments will be interest income. A second part will be your own money
—coming back to you. And the third part of that payment will be
the pay-back of the discount—the profit. Perhaps you may think
that this problem could be solved if you subtracted the portion that
is your own money coming back, deposited it in a separate account,
and used it only for reinvestment. In theory, this would be a good
method. In practice, however, you would always be combining
your returned money with your surplus from other ordinary income for new investments. Before long, you would lose track of
which funds were which.

It took me more than ten years to work out a satisfactory system of bookkeeping that was a correct financial record—simple
enough to be managed without outside help and suitable for both
income tax returns and my own appraisal of my activities. I will
explain it in some detail.

● THE MONTHLY STATEMENT

The important part of my system is a monthly financial statement to show the net worth of my investment business. I work
these statements out on the tenth of each month, a date that is
spaced far enough beyond the first so that my previous month's
salary has been paid, my bills are paid, and most of those installment payments due on the first have come in. I then compare my
net worth with that of the previous month to determine my net
gain for the month. Here is a sample of such a financial statement
with the mortgages listed by street addresses:

Col. I	Col. II	Col. III	Col. IV
Titan St.	$ 52.16	$10,432.00	$10,432.00
Bonhomme St.	48.76	7,500.00	7,802.14
Garden Ave.	39.05	6,500.00	6,942.20
Chester St.	19.47	3,894.54	3,894.54
Fortune Ave.	20.02	3,432.04	3,432.04
Corrigan St.	18.85	2,500.00	3,142.15
W. 57th St.	17.92	2,200.00	2,987.32
Glen Cove Dr.	14.47	1,800.00	2,412.18
Mirador St.	11.56	2,312.50	2,312.50
W. 89th St.	8.93	1,300.00	1,487.53
Farcrest St.	6.94	1,000.00	1,189.60
Worth St.	4.57	784.10	784.10
	$262.70	$43,655.18	$46,818.30

Less Loans Payable

Bank	9.33	1,000.00
Private	3.30	600.00
Subtotal	12.63	1,600.00
Net	$250.07	$45,218.30

Less Reserve for Mtg. Losses ($3,163.12) $3,360.00

True Value of Mortgage Investment $41,858.30

Stocks and Bonds

L. Bond	$4.58	$720.00
S. Bond	4.17	900.00
P. Stock	45.00	7,950.00
H. Stock	20.00	3,050.00
R. Stock	5.33	960.00
	$79.08	$13,580.00
Less Reserve for Adj. of Cost to Market		$600.00

Value of Stocks and Bonds $12,980.00

Current Funds

Savings	$9.00	$2,742.00
Checking		623.17
Totals	$338.15	3,365.17
		$58,203.47

General Reserve (Taxes and Insurance)	$753.42	
Car and Furniture Reserve	1,425.00	2,178.42
Net Worth....................................		$56,025.05

(You will note that I do not list my home, cars, or other personal belongings in this financial statement but I do subtract the projected personal expenditures—car and furniture reserve—before establishing my net worth. I think this is the most accurate method of handling personal consumer items, which produce no income but do constitute a future withdrawal from financial resources.)

According to the above statement, my net worth comes to $56,025.05. I look back to the previous month and find that my net worth at that time was $55,735.97. I have gained $289.08 over and above all my business expenses, all my personal expenses and all annual and long-term expenditures.

● THE EXPLANATION

Let me go back and explain the items in this financial statement, with particular reference to the listed mortgages. Column I, obviously, is the identification of mortgage investments. Column II gives the amount of mortgage interest in the first section (and monthly rate of dividends, bond interest, and savings account interest in the lower section). The total of this column is my estimated income from all investments for the month. Column III is my best judgment as to the figure at which each mortgage will become completely safe and loss-proof, even if a default and resale becomes necessary. If I consider the particular mortgage completely secure, I carry it at the current balance, the same as that shown in Column IV, which lists the balance due on each mortgage as shown by my copy of the payment book. The figures listed in Column IV are the amounts which must be paid by the various homeowners, but are higher than the price I paid for them.

To cover the inflated figure (above my discounted cost), I carry a reserve for mortgage losses ($3,360 in the statement) which is reduced every month by a figure that approximates the actual discount pay-back profit. In the particular month shown, my discount pay-back profit figures to be $44, while my deduction from my reserve was $40. I was deducting a few dollars less than the true figure because I do not take the time to calculate the discount pay-back every month. Since this profit rises every month, and my deduction from reserve remains at the same figure for several months, the reserve for losses is always conservatively safe. In a short time, when the monthly profit reaches $45, I will start subtracting $45 from the reserve.

When I buy a new mortgage, I put it on my financial statement at face value and add most of the discount to the reserve. Thus, my net worth, which is stated after deducting that reserve, is accurately specified on a mortgage cost basis. In order to check the adequacy of my reserve, I subtract the total of Column III from the total of Column IV. If the difference between the safe valuation for the investments and the current total of balances is less than the reserve, everything is fine. In the statement presented above the difference comes to $3,163.12, well below the $3,360 reserve.

● I ADD A NEW MORTGAGE

To make this record system clearer, I will illustrate my method by adding a new mortgage to the statement and then giving the complete monthly statement of the following month.

I buy a seasoned 7% second mortgage which has a principal balance of $2,402.15. Since I get a 15% discount, $360.32, I pay $2,041.83. I add this investment to my financial statement, listing it by its location on Grace Road and entering the full amount of the balance due, $2,402.15, as an asset. After a bit of consideration, I decide to give myself a little of the discount at once, partly to cover purchase expenses, partly to catch up with profits I have not yet taken on other mortgages. So I add $300 to my reserve. (The actual addition to reserve comes out at $260 because I must remember the regular $40 monthly reduction.)

I also have to decide what figure to use in Column III. Although I consider this investment very safe, I haven't yet received a payment. Being unsure about this figure, I put it down at the approximate cost and make a mental note to correct this later.

● **THE SECOND MONTH'S STATEMENT**

Here is my complete financial statement for the following month:

Col. I	Col. II	Col. III	Col. IV
Titan St.	$ 52.02	$10,404.16	$10,404.16
Bonhomme St.	48.60	7,500.00	7,775.90
Garden Ave.	38.85	6,500.00	6,906.25
Chester St.	18.95	3,789.01	3,789.01
Fortune Ave.	19.90	3,412.06	3,412.06
Corrigan St.	18.75	2,500.00	3,125.00
W. 57th St.	17.79	2,200.00	2,965.24
Glen Cove Dr.	14.44	1,800.00	2,406.65
Grace Road	14.01	2,040.00	2,402.15
Mirador St.	11.37	2,274.06	2,274.06
W. 89th St.	8.83	1,300.00	1,471.46
Farcrest St.	6.87	1,000.00	1,178.04
Worth St.	4.45	763.67	763.67
	$274.83	$45,482.96	$48,873.65

Less Loans Payable

Private	3.30		600.00
Net	$271.53		$48,273.65

Less Reserve for
Mortgage Losses ($3,390.69)   3,620.00

True Value of Mortgage Investment $44,653.65

Stocks and Bonds

L. Bond	$ 4.58	$ 720.00	
S. Bond	4.17	900.00	
P. Stock	45.00	7,950.00	
H. Stock	20.00	3,050.00	
R. Stock	5.33	960.00	
	$ 79.08	$13,580.00	

Less Reserve for
Adjustment of Cost to Market $600.00

Value of Stocks and Bonds $12,980.00

Current Funds

Savings	2.00	792.18	
Checking		401.10	
Totals	$352.61		1,193.28
			$58,826.93

General Reserves (Taxes and Insurance) $ 903.42
Car and Furniture Reserve   1,485.00   2,388.42

Net Worth...................................... $56,438.51

I am pleased with this result. I have gained $413.46 and I have increased my monthly interest and dividend income from $338.15 to $352.61. There will be an increase in profits too, from the previous $44.40 to about $50.

● MY NET INCOME

When I say, at this point, that I have virtually finished my explanation of my bookkeeping, you may not believe me; an expert accountant might go so far as to declare that I have only a series of financial statements and no real system of books at all. I don't mind. It works for me and tells me whether I am gaining or losing. If that accountant (knowing how my personal expenses can cause considerable variation from month to month) asks me to give him an exact figure of my monthly net income from investments, I can surprise him with an immediate answer.

Here is how I do it. I already have at hand the monthly total of interest and dividends—the Column II total. To this I merely add the total of discount pay-back profit (which is the amount I am subtracting from my reserve each month). This is my net income, which will usually be within $5 of the correct figure.

If I want to be exact to the cent I need ten minutes, for I must multiply the principal portion of each installment payment by the appropriate discount rate to get the pay-back profit on each mortgage. Then I total them and add that total to my Column II total. As I stated earlier, the discount pay-back profit was $44.40 at the time of the first financial statement. After the addition of the new mortgage, with a $50 monthly payment containing a $35.99 credit to principal, I can add $5.40 to my discount pay-back profit. Since there was a monthly increase of 18 cents in the older mortgage profits, the new and precise profit figure is $49.98. Thus, my exact monthly net income from my investments would be $402.59.

The fact that there is a discrepancy between the net gain for the month ($413.46) and my net income from investments ($402.59), simply means that our family expenses were about $11 less than my take-home pay.

● CASH FLOW

There is another kind of calculation you may have to make when you are thinking of buying another mortgage and are a little short of cash. You plan to arrange for a loan, but you want to know how much of a loan you will need and for how long. You make a cash flow calculation for a two- or three-month period. This is quite simple and can be worked out on a scrap of paper in a few minutes. Add up your take-home pay, the installment payments you will be receiving, your dividends, and other income for the period you have set. Then subtract your expenses, allowing a little extra for something you might have overlooked, and you have the amount of cash you will have on hand to repay your obligation.

● RECORDS

Although it is more important for your income tax than for your bookkeeping, let's mention your record of expenses. You will, of course, be keeping good checkbook stubs, properly dated. As an added precaution, you should note which checks are for expenditures connected with your mortgage business.

It is even more important to keep a diary. Note down the mileage of all auto trips that have anything to do with the business of purchasing mortgages and collecting the payments. These entries should give enough information so you can demonstrate, at a later date, that the trip was to check up on a mortgage you might wish to buy or that it was required to aid in the collection of a late payment. *Be sure to enter every trip*—to the bank to deposit payments or arrange for a loan; to the stationery store to buy envelopes; to the post office to buy stamps or to the mail box to drop off one of your debtor's payment books; to a mortgage broker; to a homeowner to see how he is keeping up his property. (Do not be like the thousands of simple people who collect $37.65 on their savings account and fail to deduct the $40 in car expense required to drive to the bank to make their deposits and withdrawals.)

Your diary will also have an entry of the date on which you made a down payment to buy a mortgage, an entry of every small cash purchase for your mortgage activity—a pen, a receipt book, writing paper, a long-distance telephone call to a delinquent homeowner. It will also contain other notations: an oral contract with a broker, a homeowner's promise to pay a late payment at a certain time, your opinion of property values in a certain district.

● MY HOMEOWNER FILE

You should have a file of envelopes or folders containing your copies of the mortgage payment books and any current correspondence with the particular homeowner. It is from these up-to-date records that you get your figures for your monthly statements.

Before we discuss these files and payment books, let me tell you how I handled the original mortgage I purchased. When I received the legal documents, I spread them out and checked the signatures and legal descriptions. Then I made sure that the payment book contained all necessary information about the homeowner—name, address, and telephone number. I put this information on the outside of a large envelope, put the payment book inside, and tucked it away in a drawer.

In later years, I have added one more item to the payment book cover—the discount percentage figure—and many other items to the outside of the envelope. One of my mortgage envelopes now contains the following information: name of homeowner and his wife; their address; telephone number; date of payment; rate of interest; due date of loan; name of the savings and loan company holding their first mortgage; and the loan number of that first mortgage. I then put all the additional information about the first mortgage—balance due, rate of interest, and amount of monthly installment—on a separate piece of paper. This goes into the large envelope and will be taken out every month to update that first mortgage by my own calculation of the amount paid on the principal. On a second piece of paper, I note down the homeowner's customary method of payment (cash, money order, or personal check, including name and address of bank). I put these two papers and the payment book into the large envelope and file the envelope in a drawer by payment date, so that the first envelope is always the one that is due or past due. The legal documents go into a separate large manila envelope for safekeeping—in a safe deposit box or safe.

● PAYMENT BOOK ENTRIES

With our current bookkeeping system complete, I will make a few remarks about payment entry procedure. When a payment arrives, I put the amount of the remittance on the homeowner's letter. Then I get out my filed envelope and put both payment books (his and mine) on my desk. I make all entries in my copy first. I calculate the monthly interest and enter it in ink. Then I subtract the interest from the payment amount and enter the principal portion, which is then subtracted from the old balance to get the current balance.

I then calculate the monthly interest on this new balance (which will be the amount of interest that the homeowner will owe me a month hence) and enter it lightly in pencil. This interest, not yet paid, is the information I need for Column II of my financial statement and it serves as a check on the arithmetic I will be doing a month later.

With my own records complete, I now take care of the receipts for the homeowner. I copy the record of the current payment into the homeowner's payment book and copy it again on a receipt that goes back to him with his book. This will give him a second record for himself while his payment book is in the mail a month later.

● CALCULATING INTEREST

There are three ways to figure monthly interest. One is the old-fashioned way of multiplying the balance by the interest rate and dividing that total by 12. A second is to use the tables you will find in payment books. The third method is to use the monthly factor, which is the interest rate divided by 12. I do not use the tables in the payment book because the monthly factor method is usually easier. On a 6% rate, with a factor of .005 or .00½, you simply move your decimal in the principal balance two places to the left and divide by 2. On a 7.2% rate, the factor is .006, which tells you to multiply by 6 and move your decimal three places to the left. Thus a principal balance of $2,420 has a $12.10 interest charge for a 6% rate and a $14.52 interest charge for a 7.2% rate. The 6.6% rate gives us a monthly factor of .0055, which I call the half-and-half rate. (You divide by two twice, with the second result moved to the left one place and added.) When the interest rate is such an oddity as 7 ¾% or 8 ½%, I do the problem the long way. I also use the old-fashioned method for 10% loans because it is only a case of moving the decimal one to the left and dividing by 12.

Get out your pencil and paper and do these problems with me:

Calculating the interest charge of $2,420 @ 6%.

By arithmetic   By the monthly factor

$$\begin{array}{r} \$2,420.00 \\ .06 \end{array}$$

$$12\,\overline{\smash)145.20\ 00}\ \big|\ \$12.10$$
$$\underline{12}$$
$$25$$
$$\underline{24}$$
$$12$$
$$\underline{12}$$

$2,420.00

$$2\,\big|\,\underline{\$24.20}$$
$$\$12.10$$

Calculating the interest charge of $2,420 @ 7.2%.

By arithmetic   By the monthly factor

$$\begin{array}{r} \$2,420.00 \\ .072 \\ \hline 4\ 840\ 00 \\ 169\ 400\ 0 \end{array}$$

$$12\,\overline{\smash)174.240\ 00}\ \big|\ \$14.52$$
$$\underline{12}$$
$$54$$
$$\underline{48}$$
$$62$$
$$\underline{60}$$
$$24$$
$$\underline{24}$$

$$\begin{array}{r} \$2,420.00 \\ .006 \\ \hline \$14.52 \end{array}$$

Calculating the interest charge of $2,420 @ 6.6%.

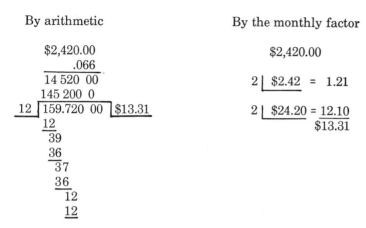

By arithmetic   By the monthly factor

Calculating the interest charge of $2,420 @ 10%.

Knowing that most of my homeowners are not experts at their bookkeeping and financial affairs, I do all I can to be exact and helpful. As mentioned above, I double-check all my interest calculations. I send all homeowners a self-addressed envelope, and I put a stamp on the self-addressed envelopes for a few of the slow payers. At the end of the year, when I total up my own record of their interest payments, I send them a copy for their income tax return.

● I WOULD NEVER ADOPT THE AMORTIZATION TABLE PROGRAM

I know that prepared amortization tables can be obtained—and that they are used in many places, but I follow the general California practice of two payment books, with the homeowner's book going back and forth between borrower and lender. I would never dream of switching to an amortization table setup because I would lose the flexibility discussed in Chapter 16.

15

YOUR INCOME TAX

● I WORKED TOO HARD

For many years, because of incorrect advice, I went to a great deal of trouble to separate my expenses according to the source of my receipts—royalties, bond interest, dividends, and mortgage investment income. As a writer, earning regular royalties, I was already keeping a careful record of my writing expenses. Later, when I bought dividend-paying stocks, I began to list the few expenses necessary to produce that income. Still later, when I got into mortgage discounting, I went into a perfect frenzy of expense separation on the basis of the threefold character of the installment payments I received. I capitalized my expenses in the period of the investigation and negotiation prior to purchase and worked out what I called the true discount. Then I tried to pro-rate my collection expenses according to the interest income and the discount pay-back profit that came in with the monthly payments. In the end, I found out that this separation and pro-rating was all wasted effort. Except for my own special expenses for writing, no complicated separation of expenses on the basis of the source of the income was required.

● THE WORD FROM THE I.R.S.

According to the representatives of the Internal Revenue Service, reports on mortgage discounting income are quite simple. The key to this simplicity is the following quote from their comprehensive booklet, "Your Federal Income Tax":

"Certain ordinary and necessary expenditures paid or incurred for the production or collection of income . . . are deductible if you itemize them in Schedule A (Form 1040).

The expenses must be directly related to the income or income-producing property and the income must be taxable."

All you have to do is keep a record of all expenses involved in your mortgage discounting activities, itemize them, and list them under Miscellaneous Deductions in Schedule A of Form 1040 (except interest paid out, which is entered under the heading provided for that expense on the deduction page). If you have kept careful records (in your diary and checkbook) you won't have to work too hard to prepare this expense report, which will probably come out as a separate, attached sheet of items, with the total transferred to the Miscellaneous Deductions line on your Form 1040.

● EXPENSES

I can't tell you what your expenses will be, but I can tell you the various items I list. My biggest item now is office rent, because I am sufficiently involved to require full use of one room of my home as an office. (I formerly charged a nominal sum for the part-time use of space in my residence, where I kept my typewriter, desk, files, and other records.) The next biggest item is car expense, which is calculated on a precise record of all mileage for mortgage activity at 10 cents a mile. (I doubt if a mortgage investor would ever reach the 15,000-mile figure that requires him to reduce the per-mile rate.) Postage and stationery are two items that build up to a respectable figure. I report telephone expense for all business pay-phone and long-distance calls. Safe deposit box rental is another item. Fees for installment payment collection are listed. Attorney fees, to the extent that the legal service is for my mortgage business, are listed. Costs for checks, drafts, and money orders are totaled. Cost of legal and financial newspapers and periodicals that advise and report on real estate activity are included in expenses. In addition, there are, from time to time, a few items that can be added to my list of expenses according to a fair answer to the question: Did I spend this money to increase my income from mortgage interest and discount pay-back profits?

Also, as mentioned above, I charge all interest that I pay out to banks, brokers, relatives, or associates if the borrowed money is used for mortgage activities. But this does not go on the sheet that itemizes Miscellaneous Deductions. Interest is reported separately, in the place where I report one or two items of personal interest that I have paid.

● INTEREST RECEIPTS

Now that expenses have been covered, we can proceed to the two categories of income that must be reported. The first is the interest income. It is very easy to determine this. I just get out my payment books and add up the interest column in each book. As I arrive at these answers, I put them on a work sheet opposite the various homeowners whose mortgages I hold. When I have completed this small chore, I have a work sheet that lists all the homeowners by name and address with the totals of their interest payments for the year.

● DISCOUNT PAY-BACK PROFIT

The other category of income is the discount pay-back profit. This is obtained by subtracting the homeowner's principal balance at the end of the year from the principal balance at the beginning of the year. This figure, the actual amount of principal payment credited to the homeowner's debt, consists of two parts— my own money coming back and my discount pay-back profit. To determine the profit, I multiply the principal payment for the year by the percentage of discount for that mortgage. The answer is the discount pay-back profit for the year. Since the Internal Revenue Service has ruled that this income, which they call discount income, is taxable as interest income, I simply add this discount pay-back profit to the proper total of interest on my work sheet.

I will demonstrate the procedure with a sample calculation: I hold the Simpson mortgage which I bought at a 25% discount. I have already totaled his interest payments, which add up to $254.22. I now check back to his principal balance at the beginning of the year and see that it was $3,784.22. At the end of the year, it has been reduced to $3,479.55. The difference is the annual principal payment, $304.67. I multiply this figure by 25% and obtain $76.17, which is the discount pay-back profit. I transfer this $76.17 to the work sheet, placing it under the $254.22 that Simpson paid in interest. The total of these two figures is $330.39, the reportable interest income I received from Mr. Simpson.

Simpson Calculation

Interest $254.22	Principal balance at beginning of year	$3,784.22
►Discount	Principal balance at end of year	3,479.55
profit 76.17		
$330.39	Principal payment for year	$ 304.67
	My discount was	.25
		15 23 35
		60 93 4
		76. 16 75
My discount pay-back profit		$76.17
ADD TO INTEREST FIGURE		

I make the same calculation for all the other mortgages and transfer the discount pay-back profit figures to the work sheet to be added to the interest totals listed therein. I then make a final sheet, listing each homeowner by name and noting the total reportable interest income received from each. To this list I add any other taxable interest I received (from bonds and savings accounts) and add them up to get my total reportable interest income.

(It hasn't happened to me yet, but I am looking forward to the day—in this computer age—when the computer cross-check of a mortgage discounter's interest income starts the lights flashing. This is certain to happen because none of the mortgage discounter's totals agree with those of the interest deductions claimed by homeowners. A great many computer operators might dismiss this discrepancy as an error that favors the government. A few expert operators, no doubt, would recognize the pattern as indicating that a mortgage discounter was reporting more income because he was correctly adding in his discount pay-back profit. But there will come a time when an overzealous operator will send out urgent notices, asking either the homeowner or the mortgagee to explain the lack of agreement in interest totals.)

● WHEN YOU SELL A MORTGAGE

Once in a while, you may have to report your discount results in a different manner. Suppose you buy a mortgage, collect payments for a few years, and then sell it to someone else. If you sell it at a profit, you report it as a long-term capital gain (bearing in mind the six-month rule). If you sell it at a loss, you report it as a long-term capital loss. To determine the profit or loss, you subtract the adjusted cost basis plus the expenses of sale from the selling price. (I have to say it in that complex way because that's exactly the method required by the I. R. S. What you are actually doing is subtracting the adjusted cost basis from the net proceeds of the sale. I should also explain that the adjusted cost basis is simply the current balance reduced by the original percentage of discount.)

Let me illustrate this: You buy a $2,125.23 mortgage at a 30% discount. After three years, when the balance is down to $1,584.58, you sell it for $1,250, paying out $136 in broker's fees and transfer costs. Your adjusted cost basis is 30% less than $1,584.58, which comes out to $1,109.21. You add the expenses of sale to this figure and get $1,245.21. You subtract this from $1,250 to arrive at a long-term capital gain of $4.79.

● THE I.R.S. SAYS IT'S WRONG

Before I conclude this chapter, I shall mention a method of income tax reporting that is in quite general use, but which is, according to I. R. S. regulations, incorrect. A discounter, who buys a $4,000 mortgage at a 20% discount ($3,200), reports the interest income without mentioning the principal payments or discount pay-back profit. When the total of principal payments reaches the amount of his investment, $3,200, he reports the remainder of the principal payments ($800) as capital gain.

Although this is incorrect, there is a very strong argument for this method. According to the I. R. S., some bonds, preferred stocks, and other institutional securities which are purchased at a discount (other than issue discount) can be reported by the buyer as showing a capital gain at retirement. It may be, at a later time, that the I. R. S. will make their regulations consistent by requiring investors in all discounted securities to report their redemption profit as interest income. Or they will allow investors in individual notes and mortgages to report their discount profits as capital gains.

16

WHEN PAYMENTS ARE LATE

● WHO IS GOING TO DO THE COLLECTING?

Many mortgage investors think they will have no collection problems if they arrange to have their mortgage payments collected by a bank or finance company. They assume, apparently, that these institutions will conduct a forceful collection assault that will insure prompt payment of every installment.

This is not always the case. All the institution does is *accept* the monthly payment, make out a record for the homeowner, and provide a record for the investor. Some of the home mortgage companies who sell hard-money mortgages will send a follow-up letter to a late homeowner, make telephone calls, or even move toward drastic action. (See Chapter 11.) In either case, however, if the homeowner becomes truly delinquent, these institutions generally turn the problem over to the mortgage holder. This means that they handle the payments that would come in automatically; you get the headaches—a little later.

Although there may be a certain psychological advantage in having your payments collected by an agent that has an impressive corporate name, the disadvantages are so great that most professional mortgage discounters prefer to handle their own collections. The first disadvantage is the cost. You have to pay a fee for collection service (except in the case of some home mortgage companies). The second problem is the delay. You will not receive information on your payments until several days after their arrival. This is not important if the homeowner follows a prompt payment pattern. But it is important in the case of late payments, for you will not be aware of a delinquency as quickly as you might wish. The third disadvantage concerns the seriously delinquent or defaulting homeowner. The collecting agent will simply turn the problem over to you after an interval which implies that it is now time to start foreclosure action. You will find, therefore, that an intermediary between you and the homeowner (in both time and personal contact) means that you cannot keep on top of the problem nor make adjustments that might salvage the situation.

● WHEN IS A PAYMENT LATE?

Another development that may surprise you, if you become a mortgage investor, is the casual attitude of many homeowners about the payment date. As the possessor of a homeowner's note and mortgage, you realize the importance of prompt payments. You have the documents and can read the fine print that tells you that failure to make any payment gives you the right to recover your investment by taking action against the mortgaged property. In some states you can start action at once, the day after the missed payment. In other states, you may have to wait a designated time before starting such action.

Although you know this and I know this, most homeowners do not seem to realize the urgency of prompt payments—and they can't refer to the documents because they don't always have them— you have them. (They should always have copies, but it has been my experience that their copies, in a box of old papers in a cupboard or closet, are as good as lost.)

Another reason for their laxity may be the fact that they have become accustomed to a certain leniency on the part of other creditors, whose indulgence may be partly motivated by a desire for additional business from the debtor. Whatever the reason, the fact remains, few homeowners make their payments ahead of time or mail them in time to arrive on the stipulated date. As a rule, however, they do make their payments within a period extending from one day to eight days late.

With this introduction, we can now proceed to a discussion of late payments, which would be those more than ten days late. The first thing to emphasize is that we don't wish to automatically proceed against the security. If I started foreclosure action every time a homeowner was ten days late, I would have become an extensive property owner and landlord. The homes I would have acquired would have been those of the good payers as well as the bad ones, for almost all of the good payers have been ten days late at one time or another. No, I try to avoid foreclosure. As I remarked earlier, I am in the mortgage discounting business—not the real estate business. I am anxious to get those installments paid so I can rebuild my cash position and buy more mortgages. That's why I follow a planned loan collection procedure that I consider reasonably lenient.

● THE TEN-DAY RULE

If there is no provision for a late fee in the signed note, I set the allowable late date at ten days. For payments 11 or more days late, I charge the homeowner extra interest on the amount of the monthly installment, figuring the actual days late. This is only a nominal amount (5¢ on a $20 payment with a 7.2% rate that is 12 days late), but it has been effective with a few homeowners who are in earnest about keeping up their payments. It has no effect on those who tend to run late with all their debt payments or those who have serious budget problems.

● AT THE 15th DAY

With these slow payers, I follow a program that starts with the position of the envelopes in my file. Since the envelopes of the past-due homeowners are now in the first place, I am always alert to which one is late and, by a glance at the envelope, how late they are. At the 15th day of lateness I send the homeowner this form letter:

Urgent Notice

I have not received the payment on your _____(first or second)_____
mortgage, which was due on _____.
This is to remind you that failure to pay each monthly installment when due constitutes a default under terms of the mortgage and gives me the right to start foreclosure action.

May I have an immediate payment.

● THE TELEPHONE CALL AND THE FINAL NOTICE

If the payment does not arrive within a week of that notice, the homeowner's envelope is still in the first position to remind me to call him on the telephone. During this call, I expect to get a definite date for payment of the late installment. I usually do get a commitment at this time (unless there is a very serious financial problem for which special adjustments must be made). If the debtor shows no sign of cooperation, I tell him I will be planning to prepare the initial foreclosure papers. (You will note that I use the phrase "planning to prepare," which is an obvious indication that the final die has not been cast.)

On the day after the second installment becomes due, I send the homeowner a personal letter listing the two payments that are in default and setting a final date—five days later, at noon—for payment of the entire delinquency. On the afternoon of that day, if I do not receive the payment or we have not arranged a payment program, I start foreclosure action.

Before we talk about the ultimate action of foreclosure, which is indicated as the foregone conclusion of such a collection timetable, let us go back to the point of the telephone call, on or about the 25th day of delinquency. (Incidentally, it has been my experience that the late payers seldom call me.) When I make this call, I am not aiming at a foreclosure to be started ten days later. I am calling to make arrangements that should now clear up the delinquency. The homeowner, who has had about 25 days to decide what he can do, usually proposes a date for the payment of the late installment. If he does not, I suggest that we may be able to work out a solution, if he will let me know what the problem is and tell me what money he will be getting.

● ADJUSTMENTS TO FIT THE CASE

At this point, I am very flexible, seeking any reasonable payment program that will avoid foreclosure and keep the interest current. In one case, where the installment payment was $22, I suggested a stop-gap payment of $30 to cover two payments. This would pay two months' interest and give the homeowner a small credit on his principal. In another case, where the payment was $30 a month, I suggested an immediate $20 payment, to be followed by additional $20 payments at spaced intervals of about 18 days. (I sent them a schedule, which they followed for several months. They then returned to the regular $30 monthly payments.) In still another case, where the interest was less than half of the installment, I accepted one payment and marked it down to cover two months. Several times I have cut the amount of the required monthly payment (for as long as ten months), and, for several homeowners, I have changed the due date of the month to a day further away from a time at which they were paying up other obligations.

I have paid homeowners' delinquent taxes and delinquent payments on their first mortgage, adding these advances to the total principal balance in the payment book. In a very special case, I even advanced money for an auto overhaul so the homeowner would have transportation to get to work. Whenever I make advances of this type, however, I ask the man and his wife to sign an acknowledgment of the increased debt in both copies of their payment book. Also, I remember that I must not allow the resulting balance to mount higher than the original figure, which is all that is legally protected by the note, mortgage, and title insurance.

Sometimes, when I make these advances, I require an increased monthly payment to reimburse me for the money advanced. In a very limited number of cases, where the homeowner was really in a tight pinch, I have let him continue with the regular installment payments.

After a decade of making adjustments, altering payment programs, and making advances that totaled several thousand dollars, I have suffered only one loss—which I may still recover through rental and resale of a foreclosed property. In all the other instances, I have managed to maintain continuous interest payments. Although I have reduced my potential profit from discount payback by making adjustments, these losses are more than balanced by mortgagors who pay more than their required payments to clear their homes of debt. In addition, I have the satisfaction of looking back over a long period of working with homeowners who have retained their homes and their property investments.

If you have read this discussion of delinquency problems hastily, I suggest that you take time to give it very serious thought. A sensible approach to your collection problems may keep you from becoming the type of investor listed here: (1) Some mortgage investors, irritated by late payments and delinquencies, have resold what they considered poor investments at a greater discount than they obtained at the time of their purchase—sometimes unloading at a fraction of original cost. (2) Others have let themselves be washed out by taking no action when the holder of the first mortgage foreclosed. (3) Still others have stopped trying to collect delinquent payments and charged off their investments as bad debts.

(4) The final group consists of those who have foreclosed, obtained title, and then resold the property at a loss.

You will not suffer these losses if you follow my earlier advice to exercise careful judgment in your original purchase and, once you hold the mortgage, *keep on top of those payments at all times, using all your ingenuity to work things out with your homeowners who find themselves in financial trouble. You must do this before they get so far behind that they are ready to throw in the sponge.*

● FORECLOSURE

Now we come to the final discussion, the absolute default that requires foreclosure action. Because of the variation in state laws with respect to foreclosure, I will have to cover this in general terms. In mortgage lien states, the mortgagee must act through an attorney who secures a court order for public sale of the security on account of debt default. In trust deed states (with power of sale), the trustee advertises the fact that the property is for sale on account of default and then sells it without any court proceedings. There is always a redemption period that allows the homeowner to make good the default and recover the property.

In my own experience with foreclosure, I have found that there are two final conclusions. When the homeowner is either unwilling or absolutely in no position to cure his default, the property is put up for sale and my total unpaid balance on the note—plus advances, interest, and foreclosure costs—acts as a cash equivalent bid for the property. If no one else makes a cash bid higher than that figure, the property becomes mine. I would now own a house that is worth about what my investment had been or one that is worth somewhat more than my original investment. It would never be worth a great deal less—because I would never have bought the mortgage in the first place. And it would never be worth a great deal more—because someone would have outbid me at the public sale. At any rate, with respect to the outcome of this particular investment, I have been converted from a mortgage discounter to a landowner, a new status that is beyond the scope of this book.

The other outcome of foreclosure action can be expected more often if your mortgages are sound. The homeowner scrapes up the cash to cure his default within the redemption period. He then reverts to his former position of installment payer—but he is now a wiser person. He will usually make his payments more promptly. If he does have problems that cause delay, he will probably respond to that first form letter. If it reaches the stage of the telephone call, he will talk to you in a sensible manner.

From my own experience, I can report that an aborted fore-closure rarely converts a problem homeowner into a different person—one who pays ahead of time or one who enters the charmed circle of those who pay within three days. The poor financial bud-geting that got him into trouble the first time will plague him the rest of his life, no doubt—but he doesn't want to get into foreclosure difficulties a second time. By the time I reach the point of making the telephone call, he has reached the stage where he will rush to the post office to send that late payment by special-delivery mail.

Here is one last word about loan collection. It is unwise and unnecessary to get angry about late payments. No matter how irritated you may be, you must remember that the homeowner has problems that are more serious than yours. Shouting at him won't ease those problems or hasten those payments. If he can't or won't make his payments, don't harden his distress into angry resistance. Remember, you do hold the upper hand. Notify him, calmly, that you are going to foreclose—*and do it.*

17

DON'T BREAK
THE LAW

Anyone who collects interest from a debtor is in a business that is subject to legal restrictions of one kind or another. Since I am not an attorney, I cannot present a complete review of all the laws which might penalize the activities of a mortgage investor. However, I have had enough experience to know what is legal and what is illegal. In this chapter, I will give you a few tips that will keep you on the straight and narrow path.

● USURY LAWS

Every state has a law that gives the legal interest rate for that state. But I won't even tell you what they are, because they do not apply to investors in mortgages. The *legal* rate of interest is only a formal statement to provide the courts with a figure they may use when a case involves a debt situation that does not specify the rate of interest. In the mortgage business, of course, the rate of interest is always specified in the promissory note. Any interest rate, if it is written in that note, becomes the legal rate for the mortgage. But that written rate *may not exceed the maximum rate of interest* for that particular kind of loan in the state where it originates.

The legal point with which we are concerned, therefore, is the state's *maximum allowable rate of interest.* This figure varies from state to state and it may. also vary according to the kind of loan. Many states specify one maximum for real estate loans and other limits for late store bills, auto loans, small loan companies, pawnbrokers, private loans, etc. We are concerned only with the limits on real estate loans, which vary from 6% to about 30%. In my state, California, the maximum is 10%. In several other states, it is 12%. In other states, it may be 8% or 9%. You will have to find out your state limit and substitute that figure as I continue this discussion on a 10% basis.

You must not collect payments on a mortgage with an attached note specifying more than 10% or you will be guilty of usury. This does not refer to the *current interest,* which you will be *earning* as a result of a discounted mortgage where your investment was less than the face of the balance, nor to your *yield* as the result of such a discount. But you will be guilty of usury if you ask the homeowner to pay a rate of interest higher than 10% on the amount of the stated principal balance of the note.

Since I am introducing you to the discounting operation, let us take an exaggerated example to demonstrate this more clearly. You pay $600 for a second mortgage, with a balance due of $1,200 that carries an 8% rate. The homeowner pays you $8 interest on the first month's payment. You are *earning* a current interest rate of 16% and a fantastic yield of perhaps 30% or 40%. But you are not guilty of usury because that debtor is *paying* only 8% of the $1,200 balance, less than the 10% legal maximum. If, because of some reason that seemed legitimate, you insisted on $10.50 to be applied as interest on that first month's payment, you would be forcing that homeowner to pay 10.5% interest and you would be guilty of usury.

There is another situation that could lead to a violation of the usury law. Suppose you originated a mortgage loan or renewed a complete new loan setup with an old debtor at 10% and then charged several hundred dollars as fees for appraisal, credit check, closing costs, etc. You would be guilty of usury, unless you could prove: (1) those expenses were necessary, and (2) that you had paid out the money to an appraiser, credit bureau, escrow firm, etc.

. I have heard of a situation in the hard-money mortgage business that is usurious: a large investor, who buys a great many 10% mortgages from a home mortgage company, receives a cut on the fees charged by the home mortgage firm. He is receiving more than the 10% maximum permitted by law. He is guilty of usury.

The stigma attached to usury should be enough to keep most people from trying to squeeze the last drop of blood from the home-owner-debtor. However, there are people who might be tempted to break their maximum interest law, so I will tell you about the penalties. In California, you can be taken to court and lose the works—the total principal and interest of that mortgage invest-ment. In other states, there are other penalties, which you should investigate if you are thinking of aping old man Scrooge. (The general intent of all state laws is to make you pay through the pocketbook by loss of interest, loss of a part or all of the debt prin-cipal, payment of all court costs, treble damages, etc.)

A mortgage discounter can make plenty of money legitimately, without violating the maximum interest restrictions of his state.

● REGULATION OF REAL ESTATE SECURITY CONCERNS

I think I am safe in saying that California has led the nation in adopting laws to regulate real estate loan activities. Since there is nothing in California law to limit my present program of mort-gage activity, there should be nothing to limit a similar program of mortgage investment in other states.

The purpose of the whole program of California legislation along this line is: (1) to protect the innocent investor from being fleeced by an unregulated mortgage investment concern or brokerage firm that operates on the basis of complete freedom to handle the investor's money; (2) to protect the homeowner from exorbitant fees on mortgage loans. To do this, California has set up a system of licensing all professional real estate security trading, setting up standards and regulations for realty brokers, putting restric-tions on fees charged by home mortgage concerns, and setting limits on the sale of mortgages by a private investor.

I do not make arrangements for mortgages which are then sold to others. I do not charge fees for real estate financing activity. I am not in the business of selling mortgages. So the laws do not apply to me. My activity, so far, a sort of last stand of individual enterprise, is solely that of buying mortgages and collecting the monthly payments. I am permitted to sell three of my mortgages on an individual basis. After that, I have to sell them through a licensed broker—or become a broker myself.

An individual Californian who invests in discounted mortgages and tucks them away in his portfolio should have no reason to complain about these legal restrictions. Investors in other states, with less restrictive laws, should be able to operate with even more latitude.

● SERVICEMEN'S RELIEF ACT

Perhaps this section should be printed in red to warn the unwary mortgage investor. *The federal government has a law to protect any civilian homeowner who enters military service from loss of that home if it was purchased prior to his induction into the service.* You, the holder of the mortgage on that house, lose your normal rights as a creditor until the aforementioned soldier, sailor, marine, or their feminine counterparts have finished their period of service.

I learned about the Servicemen's Relief Act in an unexpected fashion. In my first foreclosure action (which never went beyond the preliminary stage), I was told that I must sign an affidavit to the effect that neither the mortgagor nor his wife were members of any of the U.S. Armed Services (which proved to be a very long list, indeed). I signed this formidable document with a great deal of trepidation. Though I was reasonably certain a couple in their late forties could not be in any of our military services, there was always the possibility that either the delinquent homeowner or his wife had run off to join up with some obscure service activity. Then I remembered, with a surge of panic, that I held a second mortgage on the home of an army sergeant who was actually stationed at a nearby base.

You may be sure that I made a prompt and very careful investigation of this protective law. The first thing I learned, to my relief, was that the law does not apply to career soldiers (such as my sergeant) if they were already in the service at the time they signed the note and mortgage. The law is to protect the civilian who finds his income drastically reduced by induction. If he had previously signed up for the installment purchase of a house, the intent of this Act (and of any measures in the same vein) is to protect that person's interest in his home. This kind of legislation provides protection in two ways: (1) by providing various quartering allowances or other extra payments for the inductee; (2) by barring any foreclosure sale of his previously purchased home.

Although the law keeps you from using the ultimate collection weapon of foreclosure, you should not automatically shy away from a mortgage because the homeowner is of draft age.

Again, as in almost every phase of mortgage investment, the investor must consider the character of that young homeowner. If he values his credit, he may turn out to be a debtor who will keep up his regular payments (or perhaps a reduced schedule of payments) from the extra allowances he gets, from his wife's employment at home, or from some other source. It will be the young man of doubtful character who will welcome the protection of this exemption and let you sweat it out for the duration of his service period.

The point to remember, therefore, when considering a mortgage obligation of a young couple, is that you cannot depend on the security of the property. Everything depends on the good faith and credit of that young couple.

Suppose, however, that you do find yourself in this position, with your homeowner in service and no payments being made. What do you do?

Don't give up without an effort. Perhaps you can arrange with the wife for a reduced schedule of payments that will keep up the interest. Perhaps you can find out where the young man is stationed, contact his commanding officer, and engender enough pressure to have some of his quartering allowance sent to you. You should be cooperative and flexible, ready to accept whatever you can get. As I said before, the law protects him—not you. *If you receive no payments, you will have to sit out the war. You can take the preliminary steps of a foreclosure, but you cannot carry through the sale until the young man's period of service comes to an end.*

● TRUTH-IN-LENDING ACT

This federal law is designed to expose the unusually high interest rates that are charged on consumer items bought on the installment plan. Prior to the enactment of this law, it was the practice to declare that the customer was paying 6% interest when he might actually be paying 12%, or more, depending on the length of the contract. The procedure was to add $6 to a $100 item, which was then paid off in equal monthly installments. As you can readily see, you paid $6 for the use of $100, but you had the use of the $100 for only one month. In the succeeding months, your debt became less and less. In the last month of a year's contract, for example, you were paying 72% for the remaining one-twelfth of your debt. In the last month of a two-year contract, you were paying 144%.

The new law required that the customer be given a statement of the true annual interest on such debts. This opened the eyes of a great many people, who discovered that the interest on their installment payments and late bills was generally running at a rate of about 20%. This Act also required a great many corporations to do a lot of percentage calculating and send out forms that stated how much true interest they were charging.

Now that I have made this brief explanation, I can safely advise a person who buys existing mortgages to forget the whole thing. You are buying a mortgage from someone who has already set the interest rate and complied with the law. If you are the original primary lender, however, you must technically comply with the law by presenting the borrower with a statement of the true annual interest, which is almost exactly the same as the interest rate stated in the note.

The reason for my casual handling of this point should be obvious. Real estate loans, in which repayment is handled by amortized payments, are not arranged with misleading or exorbitant interest charges. The interest rate stated on the original note is the true annual interest, and the installment payment program, with interest charged on the remaining balance, insures that the debtor will not be charged unfair interest. As long as you charge the exact interest rate stated in the promissory note (which should have been correctly transferred to the payment books), you are complying with the Truth-in-Lending Act in letter and in spirit.

As pointed out in the section on usury, the fact that you are earning a greater interest rate on your cost (because of the discount) does not make you subject to legal action under either law. You can *earn* a yield of 20% or 40%, but this would be due to a discount given to you by the seller of the mortgage; the homeowner is still *paying* only the interest rate specified in the promissory note.

18

MY FRIEND JOINED AN INVESTMENT CLUB

● IT MUST BE ADAPTED

Investors in mortgages can utilize a device that has been used successfully for stock market investment, if they will adapt it for the special problems of this kind of business enterprise. I am referring to the investment club, which proliferated in the long period of the bull market and, though beset by problems in a down phase of the market, continues as a means of pooling the funds of small investors.

But you cannot move this device into the mortgage field and operate in exactly the same manner as you would proceed when investing in the stock market. So far as I have been able to discover, every investment club that has operated in mortgages on the basis of committee or group decision has failed to produce the results that the organizers hoped to achieve.

The underlying reason for those failures was the fact that the members did not

144

understand how their income was generated. Conditioned to the buying and selling that produces big profits (or big losses) at periodic intervals, they could not adjust to an investment program that is very much like depositing money in a savings account and waiting for the total to increase. Also, they could not understand an apparent contradiction: the necessity for quick decisions to obtain what is, after all, only a steady percentage of principal. They missed the fact that a high percentage on one's principal, obtained on a monthly basis, is more profitable, in the long run, than dramatic but intermittent profits. Since they did not get excited about those higher percentages, they would not adapt their program or delegate decision-making to go after those higher percentages.

● TOO MANY COOKS

Let me tell you about an investment club that never got off the ground. A group of investors asked a mortgage broker to attend their organizational meeting and explain the business of mortgage discounting. Following this talk, eight of the participants formed a group for the purpose of buying discounted mortgages. They each put in $2,000 to form a capital pool of $16,000. To direct their investment program, they elected a three-man executive committee. With their $16,000 deposited in a savings account, they were ready for business.

One of the executive committee members saw an advertisement of a mortgage that looked interesting. So he talked to the mortgage holder who had it up for sale. Then he went out and looked at the property that secured the mortgage. Satisfied that it was a good deal, he called the other committee members to tell them about the proposition. Three days later, after the other two men had looked at the property, they met to talk over the proposition. It looked all right and they were about to decide to purchase the mortgage, but one man proposed that they call the employer of the homeowner-debtor to confirm his employment and seniority. This seemed reasonable, so they postponed their commitment until the objector could make this routine checkup. The following afternoon, backed by the unanimous agreement of his committee, the chairman called the mortgage holder to tell him they would purchase his mortgage. It was too late. The mortgage had been sold to someone else.

Almost the same thing happened when they received a list of offered mortgages from the broker who had been their earlier guest speaker. Each committee member had a different idea as to which mortgage was the best deal. By the time they had all checked the properties and agreed on one of the offerings as a suitable investment, that mortgage had been sold to another buyer.

The chairman realized that they had to move faster. When the next list arrived, he picked a $4,000 second mortgage offering, obtained a 48-hour verbal option from the broker, and pushed the other committeemen to a quick decision. They bought their first mortgage, a 7.2% note with monthly payments of $40 at a 20% discount.

● MORE DISCORD THAN PROFIT

But there were repercussions from this transaction. One of the other members of the committee, who felt that the chairman had been too dictatorial, expressed his opinions to some of the club members. There was a good deal of talk about the personality of the chairman. When the chairman tried to push through another 20% discount deal, the two other men objected. Fortified by the criticisms of the general membership and armed with newspaper ads that mentioned discounts of 25 and 30%, they told the chairman they should hold out for a 25% discount. When the broker refused to increase the discount figure, the committee voted not to buy the mortgage.

Their failure to act favorably on their 48-hour verbal option irritated the broker, who felt that he might have offended one of his regular customers—a buyer who had to wait for the investment club's decision. When the chairman of the investment club asked for another two-day option, the broker refused to consider it.

After several months of existence, the investment club's record of earnings was not one to which the participants could point with pride. They owned one mortgage which produced $27 a month (after adding in the discount pay-back profit). When this was added to the interest on their savings account, they found that their monthly earnings were $80, which figured out at an annual rate of about 6%. At this point, one of the committee members raised the question of the expenses incurred by the executive committee. He pointed out that he had made five inspection trips at his own expense. Looking forward to additional car expenses, he argued that he would receive a net return that would be less than he could make if he had left his $2,000 in an ordinary savings account.

The members of the investment club decided to liquidate their enterprise. The chairman took over the one mortgage they had purchased; the other members got their original investment back with nominal interest.

The failure of this particular project should not discourage a group of investors who have a complete understanding of this type of activity. If their desire for quick, visible profit is sensibly restrained and they are willing to delegate the management to a dependable and trusted representative, they can make satisfactory profits.

● MY FRIEND REPORTS A SUCCESSFUL OPERATION

I will give you a detailed outline of such a successful investment club. This information is based on an interview with one of the original organizers of the club, who also allowed me to study their latest financial report, which was prepared by a certified accountant.

The club is organized as a legal limited partnership, with all operations carried on by one general partner. There are periodic meetings of the entire membership, of course, but they are for policy decisions and reports. They do not make decisions on each mortgage purchase, for the general partner decides what to purchase. They started three years ago with 40 partners who put in $1,000 each. During this initial period there were some partners who withdrew and others who joined, which produced a current situation somewhat different than the starting group. They now have 34 partners and a capital of approximately $125,000.

Their original plan of growth, which called for each partner to add $50 a month to his share, was dropped. Partners are permitted to increase their shares on an individual basis of new investments of varying amounts, which must be in round sums of $50 or more.

The participants pay the general partner a nominal sum for his management duties, based on a percentage of one-half of 1% of the total capital plus 5% of the gross profits of the enterprise. As near as I can calculate, this payment would now be about $1,200 a year. Out of this payment, however, the general manager provides office facilities, postage, stationery, etc. (which is not such a great outlay for a professional man who already maintains his own office. But there is also his car expense and a much larger payment which he must pay their accountant, who now receives $500 a year. The resulting net proceeds to the general partner—only a few hundred dollars a year—is, I think, a principal reason for the success of their operation.

That low payment for management is undoubtedly acceptable to the general partner because their investment policy and procedure is such that he is not too heavily burdened. In the first place, the group concentrates on hard-money mortgages which they obtain from a single home mortgage company. As the home mortgage firm makes a thorough credit check of the borrower and also obtains a professional appraisal of the real estate that secures the promissory note, the general partner is relieved of the duty of making time-consuming investigations. Furthermore, the general partner does not have to consider a great many borderline decisions because these have already been determined by set guidelines formulated by the group. These guidelines are: Loans are limited to $5,000 on any one property, the property value must not exceed $35,000, and the combined first and second mortgages may not exceed 80% of the market value of the property. Finally, the general partner does not have to handle the ordinary collections. Homeowners make their payments to an escrow company and the receipts are promptly deposited in the group's savings account.

At the time of my inquiry, the group held a total of 54 mortgages, of which 39 were of the hard-money type and 15 had been obtained at varying discounts. They had suffered no defaults, but reported several delinquencies, one of which was close to a condition that might require foreclosure. According to my friend, however, all of the delinquencies were on properties that had market values high enough to suggest the realization of an actual profit if foreclosure and resale became a necessity.

The earnings of the group for three years averaged 9% per annum, after deduction of all expenses. However, this was not the total yield because their unrealized profits on their discounted mortgages stood at a figure of over $4,500. According to my analysis of their financial report, this additional discount pay-back profit should boost their actual net earnings to a figure of approximately 12%.

On the basis of the reports of this investment club, operating as a limited partnership, we can come to a very interesting conclusion: *their members will double their money in five years and ten months.*

● WHY MY PRESENTATION IS BRIEF

I have given only a short report of the investment club operation, an account that emphasizes what I consider to be the key factor —the manner of making decisions on investments. I have avoided a more detailed discussion for obvious reasons. Any group of people who organize themselves into a joint venture of this nature must operate on the basis of the specific laws of the state in which they live, so they must get the advice of an attorney in their state.

19

APARTMENT HOUSE MORTGAGES ARE TOO BIG FOR ME

● I LOOKED AT SEVERAL APARTMENT MORTGAGE DEALS

I had acquired one first mortgage and a half-dozen seconds. All the payments were current, and I had several thousand dollars in cash. I considered the time was ripe for some kind of forward step. Why not, I asked myself, buy a second mortgage on a small apartment house? If it turned sour, my wife and I could take it over and collect the rents until I retired. At that time, we could move into one of the apartments and be right on the spot to keep busy looking after an income-producing property.

I began to pay attention to advertisements of second mortgages on income property; I checked the brokers' lists for the same kind of investment. At last I spotted an interesting offer. It was a second mortgage on a three-unit apartment house in a higher-priced area of West Los Angeles. The property had just sold for $55,000 with a down payment of $7,000. The first mortgage was for $42,000, with monthly payments of $284, including 6½% interest. The second mortgage of $6,000 called for $50 payments, also at 6½%. The second mortgage was offered at a price of $5,000.

My wife and I drove out to a newly developed district between the University of California Campus (U.C.L.A.) and the Los Angeles International Airport and found ourselves in an area where the sand dunes still showed beneath the new landscaping. (It was about 3 miles from the Santa Monica Beach.) The large houses gave the appearance of being custom built, and the apartment houses all had gimmicks to suggest special architectural design. It was, in short, an upper-class residential area.

We found our triplex and parked at the curb to inspect the building. It was built in the form of an "L," with the stem of the "L" toward the street and a driveway paralleling that part of the building. At the end of the driveway, across the back of the lot, was a large apartment which was, undoubtedly, the owner's residence. The garages were in the juncture of the stem and the base of the "L." As I considered the newly planted small trees and shrubs, which had the appearance of professional landscape planning, I saw the neat sign advertising a two-bedroom apartment for rent.

"Well," I remarked to my wife, "it looks like $55,000."

She agreed. "This is not a cheap neighborhood."

We walked up the driveway, edging past the battered panel truck of a TV service company and started for the rear apartment. But my wife stopped me.

"I think the vacant apartment is the middle one," she said, pointing to a door that was partly open. "The owner is probably in there —unless it's the TV repair man."

As I turned back, an inspiration prompted me to whisper, "Let's pretend we are looking for an apartment."

A moment later, finding both the owner and his wife at work in the vacant apartment, we introduced ourselves as apartment seekers. This pose gave us the run of the place, from the handsomely tiled bathroom to the designated stall in the three-car garage. We learned that the rent was $175 and that the new owners were very anxious to rent that middle apartment. We also learned that the new owner ran his own TV shop in Santa Monica, that his wife had stopped working because she was expecting a baby, and that the front apartment would probably be available in two months.

When we drove away, my wife was bubbling over with pleasure at this truly luxurious triplex—but I did not share her enthusiasm. As I cruised slowly about this alien neighborhood, I was searching for rental signs. And I discovered what I suspected. In this area of numerous duplexes and triplexes, every other building exhibited a "for rent" sign.

● THE YOUNG COUPLE WERE IN TROUBLE

"I don't think they are going to make it," I remarked.

"What?" exclaimed my wife. "What did you say?"

"I said they aren't going to make it."

"Do you mean that nice, hard-working young couple we talked to?"

I nodded. "Look," I said, "here is a couple who have worked very hard to scrape up $7,000. She worked to make extra money. He kept on using an old truck in his TV business. They kept driving their old Chevy—the five-year-old model in the garage. Then they took all their savings and put it into this expensive triplex, expecting that the rent would carry their debt payments."

"What's wrong with that?" asked my wife. "That's the way to get ahead in the world."

I did the arithmetic. The total of their two mortgage payments was $334. Taxes and insurance and upkeep would add another $100. So they had a constant monthly expense of $434. To cover this, they would have an income of $350 a month during periods when both apartments were rented. At the moment, with only one apartment rented, they had $175 to cover a $434 outlay. In two months, when the front apartment became vacant, they would have no income for that unrelenting $434 a month.

"No," I concluded, "unless those kids are extremely lucky, they are going to lose their nice new triplex."

"But you said you wanted to find a deal we could take over."

"That's not what I said," I protested. "I want a deal where the apartment owner can pay off the loan—but one that we would be willing to take over if he did get into trouble."

"What's the difference?"

"The difference is that this young couple is already in trouble—and we would be stealing their $7,000 down payment as plainly as if we had robbed them at gun point."

"There is something else," said my wife, suddenly reverting to her usual cautious attitude. "If we did take over that triplex, we might have our own problems with rent collections, vacancies, and first mortgage payments."

I laughed. "Now we have reached the heart of the matter," I said. "I can claim high moral principles that won't let me steal $7,000, but I'm really turning this down because I don't want to lose the $5,000 we would have to put up for the second mortgage."

● THE SAN FERNANDO VALLEY FOUR-UNIT

Shortly after that, I was offered another apartment mortgage in the San Fernando Valley. It was a $4,500 second mortgage with payments of $45 a month, including 7.2% interest. The discount was 20%, which put my cost price at $3,600, a sum I could easily raise. The property was a small four-unit apartment house which had sold for $48,500 with a $5,000 down payment and a $39,000 first mortgage. The monthly payments on the first mortgage were $275, including 7% interest.

It was nearing noon on a Sunday morning when I drove up before a narrow Cape Cod style building that ran back to a tree-shaded garage. Since there was no driveway, I guessed that there was a California rarity here—an alley behind the lot. The four apartments, which had separate entrances, could be reached by walking along a brick walkway that extended from low cement steps at the front to the garage at the rear.

As I always do, I went up the steps slowly, my eyes intent, to check the condition of the property—style and age of construction, paint, condition of roof, quality of gardening care, and general layout. I knocked at the door of the first apartment but obtained no response. After a little wait, I returned to the brick walk and strolled toward the rear. I was continuing my inspection while I considered which apartment I should try next.

● THE TALKATIVE TENANT

At that moment, a plump, gray-haired woman came out of the garage and approached me. She was dressed in her Sunday best, as if she had just returned from church (which she had). I told her I was looking for the owner of the property.

"The old owner or the new one?" she asked.

"The new one, A. L. Graham."

"She lives in Van Nuys," said the old lady. "If you want to wait a minute, I'll get her address."

"Fine," I said, walking with her to the door of the second apartment. Then, in hopes of getting a little information from a tenant, I asked, "Have you lived here long?"

"Ten years," she answered. She stopped and faced me. "But I don't talk about the owners or my neighbors. I believe in keeping my mouth shut."

"Of course," I said, "that's the best policy." I stopped, expecting her to go on into her apartment to get the owner's address.

But she was not through explaining her philosophy of the closed mouth. "It's like I tell Mrs. Wright, the lady in the next building—if the new owner doesn't keep up the place like the old owner, it's better not to be talking about it."

"The place looks very nice to me," I remarked.

"This new owner doesn't keep it up. She sends her nephew over to do the gardening, but he doesn't even rake up the leaves. And now she raised the rent on the front apartment. She made the new young lady pay $110 a month."

"I tried that apartment," I said, "but no one answered."

"I don't believe in talking about people," said my informant, "but I'm always glad when she's gone. She plays her records too loud. I've been here a long time. I deserve a little consideration. I'll admit I don't pay as much rent as she does, but I've been a good tenant for ten years."

Although I put in a word now and then, I actually spent the next 15 minutes listening to a lady "who didn't believe in talking," tell me all the details about rents, the advantages and disadvantages of each of the four apartments, and the habits and personalities of the other three tenants, the new owner, and the previous owner. Finally, overloaded with information, I had to tear myself away.

Before I started my car, I did a little calculation. The front apartment rented for $110, the next two for $90 each, and the rear one for $85. This came to a total of $375, which did not seem adequate to cover mortgage payments of $321 plus taxes, insurance, and upkeep. The new owner, who was a career secretary, would undoubtedly be raising rents on the rear apartments just as she had already raised the rent on that front apartment. In that event, she might get some vacancies. Even if there were no vacancies, she would still be operating on a very narrow margin—perhaps $425 in receipts against something like $415 in upkeep.

● THE "ROAD TO RICHES"—THROUGH LEVERAGE

Although they were really beyond my financial resources at that time, I later investigated several larger second mortgages—a $7,500 second mortgage on an eight-unit apartment and a $10,000 second on a 12-unit property. In both cases, I found the same situation with regard to income and expenses. The owners, with small equities, were operating on narrow margins, a repeated pattern that led me to an interesting conclusion. All of these apartment owners were attempting to use leverage to "get rich."

The principle of leverage, which has built many a fortune, can be explained as a simple process of using other people's money.

If a person has a salaried income that will support him, he takes his small savings of a few thousand dollars and buys an equity in an income property. The property must have enough gross income to cover a heavy burden of multiple mortgages and ordinary maintenance. The new apartment owner is short on working capital and gets no spendable income, but he cuts his income taxes on his salaried income and the principal payments on the debt will eventually provide him with a substantial debt-free piece of income property.

That's what happens if everything goes well. If he has trouble—from a possible combination of heavy expenses, many vacancies, too many poor tenants, and unexpectedly high property taxes—he loses his shirt. And this is the point that concerns us—when he loses his shirt, he generally cripples the low man on the mortgage totem pole. The junior mortgagee, at considerable expense, will now have to shoulder the burdens that sank the overambitious apartment house owner who had his heart set on becoming a millionaire.

I decided to abandon my incipient program of discounting apartment house mortgages. In addition to the reasons already indicated—the speculative character of these small deals and my own lack of capital for better and sounder large mortgages—I came up with a new purpose. As outlined in Chapter 12, I would program my activity to move up to first-mortgage investing.

● TIPS FOR THE INVESTOR IN INCOME PROPERTY

My own decision to avoid apartments should not deter you. You may have more money than I had; you may run into much better opportunities than I encountered—so don't let me stop you. There is money to be made in mortgages on income property; there is the kind of profit on income property enjoyed by a Hollywood broker I interviewed. He has a portfolio of about 40 apartment mortgages on which there has never been a default.

If you do plan to enter this area of investment, I suggest that you consider some general advice I can present here. Remember that anyone can get into the business of buying mortgages on single-family, owner-occupied homes. Almost anyone can be an amateur appraiser of a house that is the security for a mortgage, because they own or rent their own home and have shopped for houses. They can be a judge of human nature, credit habits, and family budgeting because they and their friends follow these same life activities.

With apartment mortgage investing, however, you move into an area that requires a knowledge of the apartment house business.

Appraising an apartment house requires a three-way approach: it can be appraised on the basis of the going market price; it can be valued on the basis of the capitalization of the income; with older, depreciated properties, it can be appraised on the basis of the land potential for other uses. You should get a professional appraisal by an independent and conservative appraiser.

When you try to judge the ability of the owner to carry his debt, you must not rely on your opinion of his character. In the case of a home, the owner's good intentions, buttressed by all kinds of social assistance, can almost always be translated into an ability to service that home debt—but the good intentions of an apartment house owner will not pay off a debt when disaster strikes. You, as a lender to an individual in a business, must appraise that individual's financial situation and audit (as it were) the books of his business.

Assuming that the owner is not a person with extensive financial resources, you should find out if he knows something about apartment management. You should determine whether he can handle his own maintenance (because the high cost of craftsmen in the field of building repair can easily turn a profitable apartment venture into a disaster).

You should consider the vacancy factor—and for this, you don't take the broad statistics of the entire city. You must know the vacancy percentage of the particular area where the apartment house is located. You must also consider the vacancy situation of the particular kind of housing that apartment building contains. If the owner has ten one-bedroom apartments, you must know if there is a surplus or a shortage of one-bedroom apartments in that district.

What about the cost of the building in relation to the general neighborhood? If the apartment is a new and expensive building in a cheap, run-down area, the owner will be unable to get tenants who will pay the higher rents necessary to keep his operation going.

In other words, you, as an investor in an apartment mortgage, must know the business almost as well as the apartment owner.

There is one very important consideration in the apartment investment field—there is a great deal of financing of sound, well-managed, profitable income property. But these mortgages are generally in the hands of large institutions or wealthy and experienced investors. The mortgages that are offered on the market tend to be: (1) those on small, new, overpriced apartment houses which appeal to the inexperienced seeker of fortune; (2) obligations of apartment house owners who are in trouble and lack working capital; and (3) liens on deteriorated apartments in poor areas where the problems of rental payments and heavy maintenance costs are a constant threat to the financial stability of the owner.

● DON'T SAY I DIDN'T WARN YOU

As I write these cautionary words, I am reminded of the cynical critic of other books which purport to be guides to fortune. This cynic said, "They are all the same. The first chapter tells you how to get rich. But the rest of the book is filled with warnings of all the troubles you will encounter." Even so, I cannot leave this outline of the problems of apartment house mortgages without repeating some of the horrendous tales I have heard.

There was the new owner who bought a sparsely tenanted old apartment house at a bargain price because he thought that paint and repair would make it sufficiently attractive to bring in paying tenants. Then he discovered that he had acquired a building whose walls hid a population explosion of mice and rats. He conducted an expensive year-long battle with scampering rodents before he was able to operate that building at the break-even point.

There was the unhappy owner (and his mortgagee) who bought an old brick apartment house a few months ahead of the time when the building inspectors checked that district. One of the inspectors, noticing the warped condition of the ground floor, followed up with a careful check of the bearing walls. They were bulging outward, a condition that resulted in an immediate and unalterable condemnation of the building.

And there was the new apartment owner whose inspection of the basement storage area was not sufficiently thorough. Ordinary rains produced no problems, but the first really heavy rainstorm filled the storage room with flood water. Every tenant who had anything stored in that room came up with a claim for damages.

In spite of all these dire warnings, which might deter the faint-hearted, a sensible investor may, with proper caution, buy mortgages on apartment houses. Whenever I think of the income property mortgage field, I recall my broker acquaintance and his 40 profitable mortgages. If there is a shortage of good discounted single-family home mortgages, I will be first in line to investigate any offer of a profitable apartment mortgage.

20

WORDS TO THE WISE

● THE CHOICE OF A BROKER

Since you will usually purchase your discounted mortgages through a broker, we should consider the importance of an evaluation of the broker's judgment and character.

It is my personal opinion that many investors place too much emphasis on the broker's judgment. Some of these investors, whether they are buying stocks or mortgages, seem to think their choice of a broker is the prime factor in the success or failure of their investment program. I do not agree. In the first place, an intelligent, experienced investor should not downgrade his own ability and wisdom, which may be superior to that of many brokers. In the second place, the advice of a broker may be impaired by a conflict of interest. A stock broker's opinion may be colored by the fact that his firm is "making a market" or actively promoting certain stocks. In much the same way, a mortgage broker's opinion may be influenced by the fact that he has only a limited stock of mortgages to be sold. If they are all bad ones, his recommendation will only mean that you will be buying one that is not quite as bad as the others.

● WHAT ABOUT THE BROKER'S CHARACTER?

The character of any person with whom you do business determines how much pleasure you derive from those transactions, but it has nothing to do with the safety or profit of the deal. The important thing in mortgage investing, as I have said repeatedly, is your own evaluation of the two factors that stand behind every mortgage—the character and good faith of the homeowner and the amount of security represented by the pledged real estate. If your judgment on these factors is sound, you can make your purchase from the most unreliable broker in town, *if you handle the actual transaction through a bonded intermediary in the manner outlined in Chapter 13.*

I have found it pleasant and advantageous to deal with a reliable broker. Such a broker will help me make an investigation by giving me a great deal of information about the property and the homeowner. He will tell me when he is giving me factual information and when he is giving me information passed on from others. He will tell me when the offer appears to be sound, when it is a speculation, and when it looks as if it might be a "foreclosure deal." He will advise me on legal matters concerning mortgages and real estate. He will give me an oral option that will be binding. He will, finally, if I have proven equally reliable, agree to a sale over the phone without a cent of money or a signed contract from me.

Nevertheless, misinformation (which is now politely called a credibility gap) is a fact of life. And the most reliable broker in Los Angeles reminds me of that when he adds, at the bottom of his list of offerings, these words: "We do not guarantee the accuracy of the above information."

● THERE ARE 50 STATES

You must remember that almost all real estate transactions are controlled by state laws. Thus, the information in this book is based primarily on California laws and procedures, with which I am most familiar. However, I have inserted footnotes or parenthetical equivalents to indicate language and procedure used outside of California. But these notes barely scratch the surface of variations that may be found in 50 separate jurisdictions. The first thing you must do, therefore, if you intend to loan money on mortgages or buy existing mortgages, is make a study of your own state's real estate laws and practices.

● TRUST DEEDS

Let me tell you about some of these variations. The use of a trust deed or deed of trust as the mortgage instrument, which originated in California, is now quite general. But the provisions of a trust deed with respect to the power of sale are different. In California, the trustee—the neutral third party who holds an inactive title— has the power of sale without court action, limited only by the three-month redemption period. In many other states where trust deeds are used, the trustee may not have the power of sale. In those states, the lender must go to court to foreclose. And, as I have indicated in other places, the redemption period may be anything from several months to a year, or perhaps longer.

● TITLE INSURANCE

In California and Nevada, the title insurance policy is a joint policy, protecting both owner and lender. In other states, there must be a separate title policy for each party, one for the owner, another for the first mortgagee, a third for the second mortgagee, etc. Furthermore, as indicated by an early footnote, the title insurance policy, which is now becoming quite general, may not be the correct document for protection of title in your state. Some states use abstracts of title and others use certificates of title or commitments of title.

An interesting situation is that of obtaining title in Iowa, where title insurance policies are not permitted. The standard document is the bulky abstract of title which is not really an ironclad guarantee of a perfect title. Many Iowa land owners and land investors, after obtaining their abstract of title, send it to a title insurance company in another state to obtain the added protection of title insurance.

● YOU WILL PROBABLY NEED A LAWYER

In California, with my general understanding of real estate law and the assistance of printed forms, I can sell real estate, make my own mortgage loan, or purchase an existing mortgage directly from the former owner with a minimum of professional aid. (I would buy the proper legal forms, pay for the protection of a title policy, and pay the nominal recording fees.)

This is not always possible in other states. In Hawaii, for example, printed forms are not permitted. As a result, a Hawaiian would need a lawyer to draw up the necessary legal documents. In many eastern states, notably New York and Florida, you would arrange all your purchase transactions through an attorney; the actual legal transfer of the property (whether real estate or mortgage) would occur at the technical moment of closure, which would be the time when your lawyer and the other party's lawyer met to exchange the money payment for the prepared documents.

I recently talked to a real estate dealer who had a long-distance transaction to arrange between a California client and an eastern broker. He told me that the transaction could not be handled smoothly because neither of them understood what the other was talking about. The term "escrow officer" (which I have already explained as the equivalent of an eastern real estate lawyer) was completely incomprehensible to the eastern man. The commitment of title, a term used by the easterner, meant absolutely nothing to my California dealer. They had to cut short their long-distance call and resort to a series of long letters of explanation.

I will not elaborate on this difficulty of communication, for I think I have said enough to make my point: The wise man will find out how real estate transactions are conducted in his own state.

● THE PAPER SALE

A promoter who develops a tract of new homes often handles the sale in this way: He gets a commitment from a savings and loan company to carry the first mortgages. Then he sets the down payment at a figure large enough to cover the difference between the first mortgage figure and the selling price. Most buyers, however, cannot put up a down payment as large as that. To make up the difference, the seller takes a second mortgage, which he promptly sells at a discount. There is no loss to the tract seller because he has set the sales price of the house at a figure high enough to give him a gross profit that will absorb the discount.

Let's run through this again, giving figures for the same transaction. Smith Construction Company builds a number of suburban houses at an average cost of $17,000. They set the selling price at $22,500 and get a savings and loan commitment for first mortgages of $16,500. Since none of the buyers can come up with a $6,000 down payment, the Smith Company agrees to accept a

$2,000 down payment and the buyer's second mortgage for $4,000. The Smith Company then sells the second mortgage at a 20% discount ($3,200) and count themselves fortunate to secure a gross profit of $4,700 for the house. (Their cost was $17,000; their receipts were the $2,000 down payment, the $16,500 from the savings and loan company, and the $3,200 net from the second mortgage for a total of $21,700.)

The foregoing was the outline of a normal successful tract sale. Sometimes, however, these deals do not proceed so smoothly. Perhaps the tract houses are hard to sell. With no income to cover construction loans, taxes, and sales expenses, the Smith Company is in danger of bankruptcy. In such a situation, the management may resort to a paper sale that is actually a scheme to peddle these homes to the people who invest in second mortgages.

This is the way it works. The Smith Company finds a nominal buyer (a person who will trade his name for the free occupancy of a new house for something like six months). There is no actual down payment, of course, but the nominal buyer signs for the $16,500 first mortgage and the $4,000 second mortgage. The second mortgage is sold for $3,200, as in the previous example. The seller has now unloaded one house and received $19,700 for a gross profit of $2,700.

A month goes by and the holder of the second mortgage receives no payment. He calls the nominal buyer, who promises to send the payment "in a few days." Two weeks later, having received no payment, the investor calls the savings and loan company that holds the first mortgage. They have received no payments either!

The holder of the second mortgage pays the default on the first mortgage. He then wastes more valuable time in a last effort to get money from the "homeowner." When that fails, he forecloses. In due time, he obtains title to the house.

It should be obvious that the investor who bought the second mortgage has been taken. Instead of making a profit of $800, he has spent that amount to secure a tract house with a $16,500 first mortgage. If he is sufficiently naive, he may console himself with the thought that he has secured a $22,500 home at a cost of about $20,500. In reality, however, he has paid $20,500 for an unsalable house that cost $17,000 to build.

If you wish to question the veracity of my account of this type of transaction I will not argue the matter, for the facts and figures given here are admittedly fictitious. But the fact that this sort of operation has been employed by tract developers cannot be questioned. Any real estate man will tell you about this kind of paper sale.

How, you may then ask, can an investor avoid this trap? You should guess the answer at once. Don't buy second mortgages on tract houses; or, if you must buy them, postpone your investment until you can establish, without question, that the new homeowner is a bona-fide buyer.

● THE RULE OF DISTANCE

There are other situations which may lead to trouble or loss for the mortgage investor. You can blunder into these situations and learn by experience, or you can read the guidelines and explanations that follow and say "No" to many an investment opportunity.

The first rule, which appears in most books on real estate financing, is to avoid investments on mortgages over 50 miles from the location of the investor. I would like to emphasize this rule, with a small amendment. *A small investor should limit his investments to a radius of 30 miles.*

Here is the explanation. When you are offered a mortgage over 30 miles away, you will have to drive more than 60 miles to investigate the deal. If you miss the homeowner on the first trip, you may have to repeat the drive. You have incurred over $10 in car expense for a mortgage you may not want to buy.

Suppose, however, that the trip was worthwhile; the deal looks good; you buy it and start collecting payments. Perhaps it will prove to be an investment that produces fairly prompt payments. Even so, you will be out of touch with the owner's care of his home because you won't make the long drives to see how the property is maintained.

Also, the opposite situation may develop. The homeowner may be quite late with his payments, so you have to call him on the phone. That will cost you something because it will be a toll call. If you have to make a personal collection visit, you will be putting in time and car expense at the rate of several hours and more than 60 miles per trip.

And there is the ultimate possibility that the homeowner may default and force you to foreclose. You will now find yourself acquiring a distant property with no idea of the deterioration and vandalism that threatens that house. Your car expense mounts as you try to keep your eye on the property. After the foreclosure you will be practically living in your car, running out to see about repairs and showing the place to potential tenants or buyers. If you rent the house, you will have to drive out to collect the payments and see about the stopped-up sewer or the leaky roof. If you sell the house, you will be doing a great deal of long-distance telephoning and driving to arrange the sale. You will definitely decide, too late, that the rule of distance was worth heeding.

● RENTAL PROPERTY

Another rule of mortgage authorities is to avoid rental property. I would like to modify this rule—for the small investor—by listing three specific rental properties he should avoid: (1) A property in which the owner's equity is small. This situation allows him to "milk" the property by collecting the rent without paying the taxes and mortgage payments or making needed repairs. (2) A house where the owner lives at a distance. An absentee landlord will tend to allow the property to deteriorate. He may also have more trouble keeping the place rented. (3) A run-down house in a deteriorated rental section. The only future for that kind of house is further deterioration.

However, it has been my experience that there are good investments in mortgages on rental property—but they should be considered carefully. One is the case where the rental property adjoins the home of the owner. Such an owner usually keeps the place in good repair and is right on top of his rent collections and his problem of keeping the place rented. Another good investment is the well-seasoned mortgage where the owner has such a large equity that he would suffer a heavy loss if he didn't keep up the mortgage payments. The third situation is the rental property close to the mortgagee's own base of operations, which he would be willing to acquire by foreclosure and manage as his own income property.

● THE LOW PAY-BACK ON PRINCIPAL

In the chapter on seasoning, I gave examples of low pay-backs on mortgage principal. In that discussion, I pointed out that the low pay-back could lessen the value of the seasoning. I will now discuss this danger from another point of view—its effect on the discount pay-back profit and the potential for added risk for the investor.

Let us suppose you are offered a second mortgage with a balance of $3,200 and monthly payments of $24, including 8% interest. This has a good rate of interest but a low principal pay-back. If you will get out your pencil, you will find that the payment on the principal for the first month's payment is only $2.67. Now, if you figure this out for three years, you will find that you have only received a little more than $108 on the principal. Thus, for this mortgage, the amount of the discount has no meaning. A 20% discount on this purchase means that the discount pay-back profit for three years will total about $21.60. If the discount were 30%, the profit for the same period would be only $32.40.

During those three years, the homeowner's financial situation may have suffered. You may find that your good debtor has now become a delinquency problem. You will then be very disturbed to discover that you are still carrying over $3,090 of that homeowner's debt. Again, the amount of the discount becomes unimportant. The difference between a $640 discount and a $960 discount means nothing when you are faced with foreclosure costs that may run up to $1,000.

When you are offered a mortgage with a monthly payment that allows very little to be applied to the principal, you should be extra cautious. Perhaps you should get out your pencil and cover several sheets of paper with figures as you calculate your discount pay-back profits for the first few years.

● THE DUE DATE

Sometimes, when you read the advertisements, you will notice an emphasis on the due date, or the broker may point out the advantage of a short due date. Perhaps you are offered a $2,000 mortgage at a 20% discount that comes due in three and a half years. This sounds very good. You will get a small portion of your discount pay-back profit with each monthly payment; in three and a half years, according to the written promise, you will receive the entire balance in a balloon payment that will give you all the rest of your discount profit.

The only thing wrong with this rosy picture is that it doesn't always come out that way. Usually, when the due date arrives, the homeowner tells you he can't make the balloon payment and asks for a renewal of his promissory note. What will you do?

You can foreclose, of course. But I don't think you will. You will usually let the homeowner continue with the old payments. And that means you will not get your discount pay-back profits any faster on that due-date note than on a note written "until paid." You may think you can insure some extra profit by fixing up a new note at a much higher rate of interest—but this doesn't work either —because you immediately run into the interest ceiling fixed by the usury laws of the state.

For my part, I prefer notes and mortgages that are written for a limited time. They are better than those that specify "until paid," because a few homeowners will make extra payments to avoid the final balloon payment. However, I don't run after the due-date notes as if they were pots of gold at the end of the rainbow. Too often these "pots of gold" turn out to be a beaten-up house obtained by foreclosure.

If I have a mortgage with a maturity date that cannot be met, I am reasonable about arranging renewals and extensions—always on the basis of the current interest rate and the actual costs I must bear in making that extension. Since I did not foreclose on that homeowner when he was 15 days late, I am not going to destroy his home investment because of a three- or five-year due date. I would rather continue—even if it reduces my profit—with a family whose payment habits I know, rather than speculate on discount profits on a new mortgage. As for you—you have now been alerted to the reality of maturity dates and can follow your own inclinations.

● THE AFFLUENT HOMEOWNER

I would like to mention one more danger in the business of mortgage discounting—the high-salaried homeowner whose income never quite reaches the level of his expenses.

My own experience with this type of homeowner can be briefly outlined. I bought a $2,400 second mortgage on a $30,000 house on the basis of the property value and the high salary of the owner, who drove an expensive automobile and was employed as a factory supervisor. I soon learned, however, that these marks of affluence were no guarantee of prompt payments. His payments were constantly a month late, frequently going past that stage, to the point where the final notice had to be sent and the date for foreclosure had been set.

After two and a half years of these kinds of last-minute "saves," I determined to carry through a precise schedule. I notified him that I would foreclose on the day after the second late payment was due and, acting on that notice, I started the foreclosure action. He quickly rounded up the necessary funds for redemption. Thereafter, apparently, he placed me a little higher on his list of creditors who had to be paid with reasonable promptness.

Let me underline this type of "affluent" homeowner by giving another quick sketch—the case of the successful professional man.

● THE SUCCESSFUL YOUNG LAWYER

This story starts with the transfer of Eugene Robertson, a young attorney, from the Oklahoma offices of an oil company to the legal staff of the main office in Los Angeles. His new salary was to be

$25,000 a year, which called for a reasonably good standard of living.

Upon his arrival in Los Angeles, and with the benevolent tolerance of the head of the legal department, Robertson spent a great part of his first month looking for a suitable home. He finally found the proper house, with a swimming pool, of course, in the Santa Monica area. He bought this property for $58,000 and was able to appear at the office with more regularity, for he could take care of the financing without extending his time off. He arranged a $40,000 first mortgage, a $10,000 second mortgage, and got a bank loan to cover part of the down payment.

Once that financing was arranged, Robertson tied himself to the regular hours of his office. However, financial problems kept him from spending all his office hours on company matters. In addition to the normal expenditures for clothing, food, utilities, club fees, car expenses, and so forth, he kept getting additional bills for his new house. There were the bills for the new appliances, the bills for the changes which had been made in the house, the payment for the landscape architect and the gardener, and the bills for care of the pool. He found himself spending a lot of time trying to make his bank balance cover the checks he had to write. Failing in that impossible effort, he kept his secretary busy filling out applications for new loans, while he was often on the phone trying to find new sources of cash. When he wasn't calling the finance companies, his creditors were calling him.

It may be that Robertson's superiors are satisfied with his regular attendance at the office and his heavy schedule of paper work on personal financial matters, but I am glad I am not the holder of that $10,000 second mortgage, and I hope you didn't buy it either.

● HOW WISE ARE YOU?

If you are a wise investor, you were skeptical about my "proof" in the introduction, under the section heading "How It's Done," in which I presented two transactions that indicated how one could double his money in five years and ten months. If so, I want to congratulate you. In that section, in an effort to demonstrate quickly the process by which discounting increases your income, I used the accounting method (now discontinued because of S. E. C. censure) of a large franchising corporation listed on the New York Stock Exchange. I listed potential income as realized earnings.

I will now present the results of those two transactions according to the principles of conservative accounting:

	Balance Due	Discounted Cost
The new mortgage	$2,000.00	$1,600.00
The original mortgage	1,284.00	1,027.20
Cash on hand	14.00	14.00
Potential value	$3,298.00	
Your original $1,600.00 has now become (at cost)		$2,641.20

According to this correct analysis of the oversimplified program I presented, you are exactly $558.80 short of doubling your money. This outcome may cause you to question my book title, but I am not concerned about your doubt. My records speak for themselves. I did double my money in six years; and I will prove it—with no tricks.

I couldn't have given this proof at the beginning of the book because the average investor would not know what I was talking about. The reader who has come this far, however, now understands how discounting produces higher yields, he knows how shorter maturity dates increase the profit, and he knows how bank loans can be used in a program of reinvestment. He will be able to follow a presentation that accurately demonstrates how I doubled my money in six years.

In the first place, the use of bank loans allows me to maintain a high degree of reinvestment. My cash does not pile up in a savings account; it goes back into mortgages. If we continue using the conservative rates of the earlier example, we find that this produces a yield of approximately 11½%. Thus, we will use that figure instead of the 5% for the reinvestment of the monthly payments I receive. In the second place, the average life of this type of mortgage is five years. So we will use that as the basis for the calculation of the return from the original investment.

Here, then, is the correct arithmetic for an operation that began with a $1,600 investment in a $2,000 second mortgage, paying $20 a month including 7% interest. In five years, I will have received $1,200 in installment payments. I will have earned $345 interest on these payments during that period. At this point, I will receive a balloon payment of $1,398 on the original mortgage. These three items total $2,943. I use $2,880 to buy a $3,600 mortgage (at the same 20% discount) that pays $36 a month including 7% interest, and have a remainder of $63.

In the remaining year of our six-year period I will receive $432 from the new $3,600 mortgage, and I will earn an extra $27.95 interest from the reinvestment of the $63 remainder and the $432 receipts. Here is the final statement:

	Balance Due	Discounted Cost
New mortgage	$3,414.00	$2,731.20
Cash remaining after purchase	63.00	63.00
Payments for 12 months	432.00	432.00
Interest on current funds	27.95	27.95
Potential value.................	$3,936.95	
My original $1,600 has now become (at cost)		$3,254.15

These figures, on a very conservative pair of mortgage investments, speak for themselves. It is quite easy to earn more on reasonably safe mortgages. Substitute 7.5% for the mortgage interest rates, 25% for the discount percentages, and 15% for the yield. The results will startle you.

21

A FEW THINGS
YOU MIGHT WANT TO KNOW

● F.H.A. LOANS

Although I was curious about F.H.A. loans during my early activity as a mortgage discounter, I never bothered to make a study of how F.H.A. operates. I wasn't in the market for a house, whether it was F.H.A. approved or not, and I didn't encounter any F.H.A. mortgages in my first ventures into mortgage investments. The same thing was true of V.A. loans, although I had a vague idea that the billboards proclaiming "No Down to Vets" or "G.I. Loans Available" had something to do with special home purchase privileges granted to veterans. Eventually, however, when my mortgage portfolio had grown to some size, I found myself in the market for a second mortgage on a house that had a V.A. first mortgage. I decided to make a complete investigation of both F.H.A. and V.A. loan programs.

The initials F.H.A. stand for Federal

Housing Administration, a federally sponsored semipublic corporation that guarantees first mortgages. (If you are thinking that you can now buy a first mortgage and have it guaranteed by the F.H.A., forget it. They only guarantee home loans made by large institutions.) To qualify for this guarantee, the property must be appraised and it must meet F.H.A. construction standards. A specified down payment (about 8%-12% for the ordinary medium-priced home) must be made. The total and life of the loan are regulated, and the interest rate is restricted to a figure that is generally a fraction lower than the conventional rate. Monthly payments are set at a figure which will cover interest, taxes, insurance, and a payment on the principal. (This type of payment is the one that adds the phrase "with impounds.") There are fees for the appraisal and the credit investigation of the buyer; and there is a charge of one-half of 1% added to the interest rate to cover the guarantee extended by the F.H.A. to the lending institution. At the time of the sale of the property, *there can be no second mortgage.*

As you can see from the foregoing, a mortgage discounter need not know much about F.H.A. There aren't any purchase-money seconds coming out of an F.H.A. mortgage transaction.

However, it is possible for a homeowner with an F.H.A. first mortgage to obtain a hard-money second mortgage at a later date. This means that we should sit up and pay attention, for an F.H.A.-approved first mortgage indicates a conservatively arranged loan, good security, and a dependable home-buyer. After an investigation to make certain that the homeowner's financial situation has not suffered a drastic setback, I would certainly take a positive attitude toward the purchase of such a second mortgage. And you should take the same point of view. It might be just the kind of deal you are seeking.

● V.A. LOANS

The first thing you must know about Veterans Administration (also known as Government Insured or G.I.) loans are the two basic types. The first type follows the general policy of the F.H.A. program, which guarantees first mortgages made by financial institutions. But there are some essential differences. Since the purpose of the Veterans Administration loan program is to assist veterans, no down payment is required; and the guarantee is more liberally extended. (However, they will not approve a loan guarantee where the property is manifestly overpriced or the buyer is either a bad credit risk or has insufficient income to take care of the monthly payments.)

The second type of V.A. loan is one that comes into existence as the result of a foreclosure or takeover of a previously mortgaged G.I. property. As can be surmised from the "no down" policy mentioned in the preceding paragraph, a considerable number of G.I. loans do go bad. The Veterans Administration takes over these properties and resells them in the same way as any other property owner who wants to sell a house. Although these repossessed properties can now be sold with a down payment, the reality of the market location of many of those homes produces a down payment that is seldom higher than 5%.

Again, as in the case of the F.H.A. loans, there are few purchase-money second mortgages. This time, however, the absence of the junior lien is not caused by any V.A. regulation; it comes about because of the no-down payment policy of original G.I. loans and the very low down-payment requirements on V.A. resales.

There can, of course, be hard-money second mortgages placed on V.A. properties at a later date, after the homeowner has built up a reasonable equity—and these should be considered by the second mortgage investor—but you will not place these investments in the same preferred class as secondary liens on F.H.A. properties. A program designed to provide housing for veterans without down payments—and lacking the strict F.H.A. regulations—does not indicate safety and security for the mortgage investor.

Having suggested that you must look at these seconds with a wary eye, I will now prove that there are exceptions to all rules. In a special circumstance, where both loans are well seasoned, you may find a safe deal—as I did.

Here is the story. A veteran obtained a G.I. loan on a suburban tract house priced at $18,000. There was no down payment, of course. He failed to keep up the payments, and the V.A. took over the property. They resold it for $17,000 with a $1,000 down payment, carrying back a $16,000 first mortgage. Eight years later, when the first balance was about $14,300, this homeowner sold the property for $18,000 with a $500 down payment and carried back a $3,200 second mortgage. Two years later, when the second balance had dropped to $2,700, this second mortgage holder offered his paper for sale at $1,700. I bought it.

I consider this investment safe because the V.A. first mortgage is now less than $14,000 and the property may be conservatively appraised at $18,000. Even more important, however, is the character of the present homeowners, whom I consider to be completely dependable.

I must add a few items about V.A. loans that are important to second mortgage holders.

There are no acceleration clauses in their notes. (See the section on acceleration clauses at the end of this chapter.) This is a good thing for me. If I have to foreclose, I can take over the V.A. loan without being obligated to make higher payments and pay higher interest—and, because of those fixed terms, I can resell the property more readily.

On the other hand, the V.A. does not charge late fees nor crowd the homeowner when he falls behind on his payments. With delinquencies that sometimes run to a period as long as six months, I may wake up some day to find that I have to cover a six months' period of delinquency to protect my interest in that V.A. property —enough said.

Although I am pleased with my solitary V.A. deal, I don't expect you to follow my example. When you receive your first offer of a second mortgage on a V.A. property, you might dig out this book and reread every line of this section very carefully—after that, you are on your own.

● IMPOUNDS

Many mortgage payments are set up to cover claims against the property (taxes and insurance premiums) which are normally paid by the homeowner annually or semiannually. The mortgagee estimates these costs in advance, pro-rates them on a monthly basis, and requires that the regular installment be large enough to provide for these obligations. This excess payment is credited to an account called the impound account, from which money is taken by the mortgagee to pay the homeowner's taxes and insurance premiums as they come due. In many cases, as in F.H.A. and V.A. loans, the impounds are calculated from the start of the payment program. In this way, an impound balance is built up before any tax or insurance payments come due.

In some cases, the mortgagee pays the obligations first and is then reimbursed on the installment plan, by the impound portion of the monthly payment. It is my understanding that this program is sometimes called a "budgeted mortgage plan," which may also be extended to cover appliances and such home improvements as washers, dryers, water softener systems, air conditioners, and even carpeting and drapes.

Let me tell you about my introduction to impounds. I received a notice, printed on red paper, from a savings and loan company that held the first mortgage on a home that was the security for one of my seconds. It was a duplicate of a warning to the homeowner that his taxes were in default. Furthermore, continued the notice, the taxes must be paid at once and the tax receipt sent to their office. Failure to take care of this obligation, they said, would cause them to initiate foreclosure proceedings.

You can be sure that I was disturbed. It looked to me as if I might have to pay those taxes to keep the savings and loan company from foreclosing, but I didn't want to pay them if the homeowner was taking care of the matter. I called the homeowner and got no answer. So I called the office of the savings and loan company to find out if the homeowner had taken care of those taxes.

"No," came the reply, "we have received no answer from the homeowner."

"I guess I'll have to pay them," I said, "but I don't want to send a check to the tax collector if the mortgagor is sending in the money."

The girl on the telephone, evidently sensing my agitation, quickly reassured me. "You don't need to pay any attention to that notice. It was just a formality. We'll pay the taxes and put the mortgage on an impound basis."

"What does that mean?" I asked.

She explained the workings of their program of impounds, which called for an addition to the homeowner's monthly payment sufficient to cover the expenditure they would make. I relaxed— and adjusted to a new situation where that homeowner now paid about $40 more on his regular first mortgage installments.

Sometimes, when a first mortgagee puts the homeowner on an enforced impound program, they do not spread the required extra payments over a 12-month period. I had one situation where those taxes had to be covered over a five-month period. In another case, the mortgagee required extra payments over a three-month period to repay an advance for insurance premiums. In still another case, the savings and loan company had the homeowner change over from a standard payment program to a permanent impound payment program by a signed amendment to his original contract.

As you can see, there is some variation in the way institutional mortgagees handle the matter of impounds. In some cases, in fact, they will not make any advance to cover taxes and insurance. They will simply make a demand that the homeowner cover his obligation according to the terms of the mortgage, a procedure that foreshadows foreclosure action. *As the holder of the second mortgage, you must now see that those taxes are paid if you want to protect the property that secures your loan.* You may have to pay the taxes (or insurance) and make a demand for repayment of your advance.

Thus, we come to the situation where you will be setting up your own impound program (because you will seldom demand immediate full repayment from the homeowner).

I have set up temporary impound programs several times. In every instance, except for the most recent payment of a tax delinquency on a first mortgage, the parties involved have repaid my advances and gone back to their regular monthly payments.

Here is an example of the way I do it. Norton, who is paying me $24 a month, including 7% interest, calls to tell me that he can't pay an overdue tax of $254.34. He sends me the bill and I pay it. I now add the $254.34 to the balance due on his mortgage, entering the larger total in both payment books. After making a mental addition of interest of about $10, I have a working figure of about $264. This amount, divided by 12, gives me $22, the added amount that Norton must pay to cover my advance. So I tell him to send me $46 a month. (In the rare event that he should object to this payment, I would point out that I can legally demand the immediate payment of the entire advance.)

When he sends in his payments, I credit them in the usual manner. But I make a notation each month, in my book only, to show the progress of the repayment of the $254.34.

You should be careful not to include the principal repayment of any advances when you work out the discount profit for your income tax. *There will be no discount profit on that homeowner's account until the total of his credits to principal totals the amount of the advance.*

However, if you use my recommended method of calculating discount profits, which required you to subtract the principal balance at the end of the year from the principal balance at the beginning of the year, you will not make the mistake of paying an income tax on discount pay-back profits you never earned. (I had an advance on one account—from taxes, payments on the first mortgage, and other expenses that totaled almost $1,000. There was no discount pay-back profit on that deal for over two years.)

● PREPAYMENT PENALTIES

You will sometimes see the phrase "prepayment penalty" in the advertisements offering mortgages for sale. This is a carry-over from the days of easier money when mortgagees were eager to keep their money working. To restrict the homeowner who wanted to pay off his debt quickly, and especially to keep him from switching to another savings and loan company on a refinancing deal, the mortgagee required a penalty payment (it was usually six months' interest) for a substantial payment on the principal. This clause is still being written in many first mortgage contracts and is generally included in hard-money second mortgages. But I am not interested in these provisions—most of my mortgages are bought at a discount, which means that I get my discount pay-back profit sooner if the homeowner pays off his debt faster. If I get a discounted mortgage with a prepayment penalty clause, I immediately notify the mortgagor that he can pay as much of the principal as he wishes without penalty.

● THE ACCELERATION CLAUSE

The acceleration clause is something else. It provides that the mortgage holder may demand full payment of the note if the property securing that note is transferred to another person. (This is sometimes referred to as a nontransferable mortgage.) This is a very valuable clause for the mortgage holder, since it allows him to cash out his investment at the time of the sale if he is not satisfied with the credit of the prospective buyer. A mortgage discounter would seldom be satisfied with the credit of the prospective buyer because it would be to his advantage to demand payment of the balance. It should be obvious, I think, that he would not want to pass up this opportunity to obtain the full amount of his discount pay-back profit.

Though I would be delighted if every mortgage contained this clause, I must live with the reality—mortgages without an acceleration clause. Thus, I must accept the terms written by the previous mortgagee. And I may find (as noted elsewhere in this book) that a homeowner has sold his equity to someone I have never had a chance to investigate.

The priceless jewel of a mortgage contract would be one that had both an acceleration clause and a prepayment penalty. If you ever get one of these at a discount, you can have your cake and eat it too. If the homeowner decides to sell his property, he gives you the opportunity of a lifetime. You demand payment and get your own money back; you get the full discount pay-back profit; and you receive the additional payment of six months' interest.

● RECOURSE

Occasionally, you will find a mortgage offered for sale "with recourse." This means that the seller guarantees you against loss. If the homeowner defaults and your foreclosure action leads to a loss for you, you have a claim against the seller of the mortgage for the amount of the loss. Sometimes, when many years pass before there is a default, the guarantee may not be so valuable. The seller may be bankrupt, dead, or otherwise unavailable.

Discounted mortgages are almost invariably sold "without recourse," which means that you have no claim against the seller once the transfer of the sale documents is completed. A discounter, who is in the business of making good money from high yields is considered to be a person who can look out for himself.

22

GET RID OF
YOUR PREJUDICES

● A SECOND MORTGAGE IN A BLACK AREA

Although I was brought up by liberal parents of diverse ancestry who were very much opposed to racial discrimination, I was a little nervous when I was given my first offer of a second mortgage on a house owned by black homeowners. But it was rated very secure by the broker, a fact that was also quite obvious to me. The mortgages on the house—both first and second—had been paid down to half their original figures. Since this indicated that there was ample security, the only remaining question was the character of the owners.

I introduced myself to Mrs. Selkirk, a statuesque black woman in her 50's, and told her I was considering the purchase of the second mortgage on their house.

"I didn't know Mr. Lemberg wanted to sell that," she replied.

"Yes," I said, "I understand he wants to raise cash to take a trip to Europe."

She nodded thoughtfully.

"I was told the remaining balance was $1,812.57," I continued. "Would you show me your payment book so I can confirm that figure?"

She went into another room, returned with the book, and handed it to me. I glanced at the final figure, but I was really intent on noting that all the payments on the page had been made on the first three days of the month. Satisfied with the payment record, I handed the book back to Mrs. Selkirk. "That checks," I said.

"How much discount are you getting on that second mortgage?"

"Ten per cent," I replied.

● SHE HAD HEARD ABOUT HIGH DISCOUNTS

"That's not enough," she exclaimed. "It ought to be 30 or 40."

"Why?" I asked, somewhat surprised at her remark. "I could see from your payment book that you're a good payer."

"I know that," she said, "I pay all my bills on time."

"That's the reason. That's why I can't buy the mortgage at a big discount."

"In this neighborhood, all the discounts are bigger. You're paying too much for that second mortgage."

"There's nothing I can do about that. If I don't buy it, someone else will." Then I made a little joke. "You're the cause of that; because you've been so prompt with your payments, it won't go for a big discount."

"I guess you're right," said Mrs. Selkirk, shaking her head. "If we hadn't been so regular with our payments, Mr. Lemberg would have had to sell it real cheap and we could have bought it ourselves."

"I'll give you first chance at it if you want to buy it," I offered. "I'll tell you the name of the broker."

"That would be more than $1,600," she said sadly. "We couldn't raise the money."

"I'm going to buy it," I said, "and I think you'll keep right on making the same prompt payments to me that you have made to Mr. Lemberg."

"Oh, yes," she agreed, "we'll keep on making those payments."

The Selkirks made all their payments on time, paying off the entire indebtedness in about five years. As a result they gained a rating, in my estimation, as people of the finest character and credit.

● SOME ARE GOOD AND SOME ARE BAD

I could give many examples of good credit on the part of black homeowners—or I could present the other side of the picture, represented by the foreclosures suffered by black families with adequate income, whose budget allocations are perverted by a false emphasis on the importance of being "big spenders." But examples of either type would not provide you with a guide; they would only remind you that some debtors are dependable and some are not.

These brief remarks, which I could duplicate for Mexican-Americans, Orientals, or Caucasians, should indicate that race is not an important factor in determining the credit and good faith of the family paying off a mortgage. The important factor is the individual character of each homeowner, without regard to race.

Let me repeat that last sentence, this time in italics: *the important factor is the individual character of each homeowner, without regard to race.*

That double emphasis is important—because it means that there is a tremendous opportunity for profit for the small investor who adopts that statement as a guiding principle.

Let us go back for a moment, to my conversation with Mrs. Selkirk. If you will review the dialogue, you will see that she thought I was paying too much for her mortgage; that she thought the discount should have been 30 or 40%. And she was right—with reference to most second mortgages in a black community, a Mexican-American district, or any other disadvantaged minority area. A great many of these second mortgages do sell at a 30%, or 40%, or even 50% discount, for the simple reason that a great many investors do not wish to risk their money outside of a high-class white area. It doesn't matter to these investors that thousands of white homeowners are poor credit risks, are unable to manage their financial affairs, or may suffer marital shipwreck. Their attitude is conditioned by race prejudice and traditional stereotypes. So they compete for mortgages in white middle-class areas, driving the prices up to the point where you are lucky to buy a doubtful second mortgage at a 20% discount.

Thus, I can honestly say, "Get rid of your prejudices," and buy first-class mortgages at discounts of 25% to 30% and fairly good ones as low as 40%. Examine each case on the basis of the credit and good faith of the homeowner, without thinking about the color of his skin.

● THE ECONOMIC HANDICAP

Perhaps, at this point, you may say, "I'm not prejudiced, but it is important to consider the true economic situation of the minority areas. There is race prejudice in our society, which produces a low income for blacks and other minority groups."

Your statement is correct. The average black man does earn less than the average white man, but there are several compensating factors. The man is not the sole wage-earner in that minority family, because his wife and/or daughter are also working. In addition, having lived in conditions of deprivation for generations, they may be able to live on less than an equivalent white family.

My advice, therefore, is to consider every mortgage offer on its merits. If the homeowner lives in a minority area, don't turn it down until you have assessed the character of that homeowner. As you make this judgment, you might remember this paraphrase of a statement that is current among mortgage investors, "Minority people have to live someplace."

● THE AREA MAPS

Let me now approach this situation from a different angle. It is fairly well known among real estate people that savings and loan companies and insurance companies use colored maps to evaluate different areas in a city. One color signifies a good area, another indicates a doubtful or mixed area, while a third marks a deteriorated or dangerous area. In the case of the insurance companies, these maps attempt to present—at a glance—the incidence of fire, robbery, and damage. In the offices of the savings and loan companies, they indicate the degree of financial risk.

While these maps are supposed to be based on statistics, there is no doubt that a certain amount of racial bias tends to influence the judgment that makes a particular block of minority residents suspect as an area of financial security. In spite of this defect, the maps are useful to a large organization which cannot handle each case on a truly individual basis. But it is precisely this generalization by areas on the part of the savings and loan companies that gives a small investor, who operates on an individual basis, an excellent opportunity. There will be, within a large area evaluated as doubtful on those maps, a satisfactory block or two where the small investor can find a sterling homeowner and buy a seasoned *first* mortgage at a good discount. They can be found and they are money-making prizes.

● PROPERTY VALUES

We must now discuss the other factor that stands behind the investment in a mortgage—the property that provides the security. Contrary to what many people believe, property values in minority areas are not lower than the equivalent property in a lower middle-class or working-class white area. As a matter of fact, the values are usually higher. In my opinion, the market value of a house in a black area will be $1,000-$2,000 more than the same-sized house in a white area. What is more, the house in the black area, though selling at $1,500 more than the white area house, is generally older.

It took me a little while to get this fact firmly established in my mind because of a special situation that occurs on the fringes of a minority area. In a white district next to a black area, a few black families buy houses. Some of the white owners, fearful of the black incursion, put their homes up for sale. Then the panic hits. All the whites try to sell at the same time. Prices go down. I soon learned, however, by many comparison appraisals, that these lower prices are only temporary. Once the area has stabilized, the prices go back up to their original figure. Later, as the pressure for housing creates a constant demand from a crowded black community, the prices go even higher.

Here, then, for the mortgage investor, is an unexpected boon. The security behind his mortgage in a sound and well-cared-for minority area will generally be stronger than he might have expected.

● BLACK CAPITALISTS

I want to conclude this short chapter by mentioning two black investors who have made a great deal of money in real estate in the black community. The first one, Clarence Wheeler, was a postal clerk who managed to save some money he could use as capital. Starting out with a little more than $1,000, he bought a second mortgage on a small duplex at a 50% discount. As suggested by the high discount, the owner was in trouble. When he defaulted on his payments, Wheeler foreclosed, moved into the duplex, repaired and painted it, and sold it for a profit of about $5,000. He repeated this operation with a higher-priced duplex. In about five years, he was the owner of three or four rental properties and had a good deal of money invested in other securities. After that I lost contact with him—primarily because he moved from one location to another so often that his phone-book listing was always out of date. When I do find time to run him down, I'll expect to find him hard at work remodeling a newly acquired 15-unit apartment house.

Jarvis was an intelligent and genial young black man who graduated from college and became a real estate salesman. Quite often, in lieu of a cash commission, Jarvis accepted a second mortgage. (This is a common occurrence which I noted in an early chapter. When a homeowner with a limited equity sells his house, the commission is often paid by writing a second mortgage which the new owner assumes, and this is given to the Realtor.)

By the time Jarvis set up his own realty office he had about a half-dozen of these small second mortgages. Occasionally, when he needed funds, he would advertise one of his second mortgages for sale. Little by little, he developed a clientele of investors who bought second mortgages. He then extended his brokerage business to include mortgages as well as real estate and began to act as a broker for other Realtors who had second mortgages to sell. As his capital expanded, he began to hold more of these mortgages as investments. In time, he built up a considerable portfolio of mortgages, though he would sell an occasional mortgage to some of his old customers.

About this time I ran into him at an escrow office, and he told me about a foreclosure he had just carried through to the final sale. "It was an eight-unit apartment house with a first mortgage that had been paid down to $20,000," he told me. "I had a $6,000 second mortgage that was in default."

"So you foreclosed," I prompted.

"What else," he said, shrugging his shoulders. "On the day of the sale, I went over to see who would bid for the property."

I laughed. "You were going to be right on the spot to collect your $6,000 from the high bidder."

"That's exactly what I had in mind," he said. "But it didn't turn out that way because there was no one there to put in a bid. I got that $60,000 apartment house for an investment of $6,000."

"I don't believe it," I said.

"That's exactly what happened."

"But you do have to carry the first mortgage," I reminded him, "not to mention the upkeep and the taxes."

He threw out his hands in a gesture of dismissal.

"That's what makes it such a terrific deal. The place is fully rented, with a gross of over $700. That's twice as much as the taxes and the mortgage payments."

Since that time, Jarvis has increased his income property holdings to a considerable extent. It is my guess that his present net worth would be fantastically high—certainly high enough to arouse the envy of an investor in any field, and high enough to prove my point about opportunities in minority areas.

23

I LIKE ADVENTURES

We have been talking about real estate, arithmetic, and legal matters—which might suggest that mortgage discounting is a prosaic business conducted at a desk. It has been my experience, however, that this activity is enlivened by human-interest situations, friendly relations, and special events that might truly be called adventures.

● THE CHRISTMAS CARD

When Molina's payment failed to arrive on time, I was not disturbed. His payment book showed a variation from three to 15 days of lateness. But you can believe I was upset when I got a final notice from the holder of his first mortgage. He was two months late, and they were about to file foreclosure papers. I telephoned Mrs. Molina to find out when her husband would be home; that evening I sat in their front room, listening to an account of their problem.

Mr. Molina, who had worked in an auto parts store for some time, had asked for a raise. In the ensuing discussion, things had warmed up enough to cause the angry manager to discharge Molina. He had been out of work for several weeks and had fallen behind on all his payments.

"I got another job now," concluded Molina. "And it pays better than the old one because I get commission added to my regular pay. I figure I make about $170 a week."

"How long have you been on the new job?" I asked.

"I just started—Monday."

"When do you get paid?"

"Two weeks."

"Have you called the office of the savings and loan company?"

Mr. Molina, frowning, shrugged his shoulders. "What good would that do? I don't have the money."

"They're going to foreclose. Then you'll have to pay another $100 in fees."

"I can't do anything until I get my pay."

I glanced at Mrs. Molina, who had put on her best dress for my call. Her dark face showed her distress at their financial dilemma. I turned back to Molina. "How much money do you have in the house?" I demanded.

"About $30," he guessed.

"I have some money," said Mrs. Molina.

"Count it," I ordered.

When they finished their inventory, the joint total came to about $55.

"Give me $50," I said. "I'll pay the savings and loan company the $238 to get you caught up and I'll add the $188 difference to your balance on the second."

Molina gave me $50 without mentioning their needs for food or pocket money. Then we worked out a program to cover their payments to me, which would now have to cover the repayment of the $188 advance.

In the months that followed, they have added a few dollars to every regular payment to apply on that advance. Best of all, however, was a later result. I received my first Christmas card from a homeowner. Hereafter, I shall not count a holiday season complete until I have received my regular Christmas message from Mrs. Molina.

● MY MYSTERY HOMEOWNER

When I acquired the second mortgage on the Draler Avenue property, I assured myself that the two-bedroom house provided adequate security and that the owner, a man named Fassett, would make the $20 monthly installments. My opinion proved to be correct; Mr. Fassett made every payment promptly—for ten months.

On the eleventh month, I received the payment in the form of a check signed by Helen Mason. And the payment book had the name of Helen Mason written above the crossed-out name of Thomas Fassett. I guessed that the Fassetts had sold their house to a family named Mason; and the new owner's wife, who was probably the financial manager of the household, had simply put her own name on the payment book.

If this were, indeed, the fact, there was nothing for me to be concerned about. Such a transfer was legal since there was no acceleration clause in the note. And the transfer did not affect my security because the house still guaranteed the obligation. But I could manufacture worries about a new situation in which I had acquired debtors who might not make their payments.

I went to the county recorder's office and learned that the Fassetts had transferred their property to a person listed as Helen Mason, *an unmarried woman.* That phrase, suggesting something other than the transfer of a home from one family to another, was disturbing. Who was this unmarried woman? What did she want with a two-bedroom house? Would she be able to make the payments?

I drove to the Draler Avenue address in hopes of learning something about this new homeowner. There was no one home. I went home and asked information for the telephone number of Helen Mason on Draler Avenue. There was no listing.

Although I was very curious—and worried—about my new debtor, I decided not to follow up my investigation at that time. I was quite certain that Miss Mason would be late with one of her payments. When that happened I could call on her.

Month followed month, however, and Miss Mason's payments always arrived between the first and the fifth. Lacking an excuse to interview her, I did not make a special trip to Draler Avenue. But I did make it a point to stop at her house whenever I was in the immediate neighborhood. All my calls were fruitless. She was never at home—or she didn't answer my knock.

As time passed, I began to think of her as a woman of mystery; and I gradually built up a fancied character that would fit the situation. I decided that Helen Mason was an older woman—perhaps in her late forties. She must be employed at a good salary—as a teacher, undoubtedly. It would also seem that she was eccentric —perhaps antisocial.

After years of regular $20 payments from my "elderly teacher," I lost interest in further investigation. *Then her payment arrived in the form of a check signed by a man, a Mr. Connor.* For a moment I thought I would have to visit the county recorder to see if she had resold the house. But the return address on the envelope carried the name of Helen Mason; her name remained on the payment book. I decided that Mr. Connor was a relative who was making one payment for my mystery woman—until the next payment arrived. This payment, again in the form of a check signed by Mr. Connor, was a further surprise. It was for $100, and there was an unsigned note announcing that larger payments would be made henceforth.

I was so pleased at this indication of a faster payoff that I made no further effort to unravel the life and character of Helen Mason. I simply manufactured a character for Mr. Connor—undoubtedly an elderly gentleman of means who had married a lonely schoolteacher. In a short time, as a result of the large payments, the mortgage was paid off.

When the last check arrived, I decided to clear up my six-year-old mystery. Instead of returning the cancelled note and released mortgage by mail, I wrote to Helen Mason to suggest an appointment so I could make personal delivery of the mortgage and note.

I was impressed by my visit to the house on Draler Avenue—primarily because my "woman of mystery" proved to be just the opposite of my contrived image. In reality, she was a young woman with a simple, straightforward story that suggested unusual depths of character. Here is her story:

Helen Mason went directly from high school to an assembly line in an appliance factory. She saved her wages and, aided by a small inheritance from her mother, bought her own home. Although she was far from ugly or disagreeable, she attracted few boy friends. It was not until she was in her late twenties that she met Mr. Connor, whom she married. He was an employee of an equipment rental company, and it was he who initiated the policy of increased house payments to liquidate the second mortgage. But the property remained in her name.

Although she did not tell me why she had retained title to the house, her words suggested that this was an important decision which had been settled—before her marriage—on the sound basis that the person with the courage to make that first down payment and shoulder the burdens of mortgage payments and taxes was the person who was entitled to the house. After our conversation, I knew that Helen Mason Connor would always hold title to that house. She had bought it—and she had the strong character, in spite of a limited education and a quiet demeanor, that would keep that one important possession—her very own home.

● INSIDE INFORMATION

The sale notice on the probate listing board interested me. A $4,600 note, reduced from an original figure of $5,300, secured by a house on West 58th Street, was offered for sale in an estate case. Although I didn't have anything like $4,600 available, the address intrigued me. That house was less than a block from Selkirk's home. Since my investment in the Selkirk mortgage, now paid off, had turned out so well, I was open to anything like it. And I knew the area quite well. I could already visualize the section—small rentals and owner-occupied homes on half lots in a neat black neighborhood. There was no question about it. I had to take a look at the property.

As I expected, the house proved to be quite small, very old, and in poor condition. The rear building that served as a garage was ready to collapse and the backyard was littered with trash. The house itself was vacant. The only favorable factor, I discovered, by looking in the windows, was an interior which had been cleaned up and newly repainted. Shaking my head at the low value of this run-down security, I returned to the front of the place and started for my car.

At that moment a young man, who had just arrived in a power company truck, intercepted me. "Do you own this house?" he called.

I shook my head. "I was just appraising it," I replied.

"I have an order to turn on the electricity," he explained. "And there's supposed to be someone here."

"I guess that would be Mr. Hinman. He's the owner."

The utility man looked in his book. Then he shook his head. "No. The customer's name is Brown. Philip Brown."

"That must be a renter," I said.

The utility man shrugged his shoulders and went across to put a tag on the front door. Then he returned to his truck and drove away, leaving me with an interesting train of thought. Chester Hinman owned a rental property worth about $7,000. It was rented to Philip Brown, who was about to move in. In a sense, I had inside information, for I knew more than any other potential investor, who might see only a run-down, empty house. Thus, I might be in a better position to make a bid for this mortgage.

But I didn't make a decision without a little more investigation. I would have wished to talk it over with the Selkirks, but I knew they had sold their home and moved into a larger house in Baldwin Hills. So I crossed the street and struck up a conversation with a young lady who had been interested in my survey of the vacant house. Being only a renter herself, she could not tell me what houses on that street were worth. But she did know rental prices. "I pay $115," she said. "Some of the other houses rent for $125."

"That seems high," I said. "These houses are all small."

"But you were looking at that old house across the street," she reminded me. "That man only gets $90."

"You seem sure of that."

"Sure, I'm sure. I asked the man."

I thanked the lady and went back to my car. As I drove back uptown, I did quite a bit of figuring. As a seasoned first mortgage, this deal might call for a bid of close to $4,000 (15 to 18% off)—if the investor considered the property was good security. But anyone who came down and found the house vacant might not consider the property such good security. Since they might not discover that the house was rented for $90, I could expect that the actual bids would be in the area of 25% discount—or there was a chance that someone might put in a bid of a flat $1,000 off, which would come out at about a 22% discount. From this logical train of thought, I decided that a bidder who wanted the deal would have a reasonably good chance of getting it at a 20% discount.

Before making up my mind, however, I had to solve another problem. I didn't have any ready cash. I then considered the time element, which is always a feature of estate bids. Judging that the probate proceedings would take two months, I did a quick calculation of my cash flow and came up with a figure between $2,500 and $3,000. Since this would be only $1,000 short of what my bid would be, I decided to submit my bid at a 20% discount.

My offer of $3,680 was the successful bid for the $4,600 first mortgage. (This investment produced a 12% yield.)

● MY FAMILY

I have been accused of exhibiting more interest in my homeowner-debtors than I do in my own family. If, by family, my cousins and nephews and nieces are meant, I must confess that there is a certain amount of truth in this accusation. After my immediate family and my very close friends, the greater part of my group of homeowners who contribute to my income have become my friends and pseudo-relatives.

I have come to know the husbands and wives and all their children. I have a pretty good idea of their incomes and their expenses. I advise them about investments, insurance, taxes, and home remodeling plans. When they are in trouble I try to help. On the other hand, when they are very late with their payments, I get irritated—in exactly the same way that I am sometimes irritated with family members who do not meet their obligations. But the interesting part of this relationship is that it is, I believe, reciprocated. Many of my homeowners definitely consider me a sort of elder brother or uncle. In one particular instance, I am almost certain that my visits represent the principal social activity of a lonely, low-income family.

When the state granted a special homeowner's tax exemption, Mrs. Rivera called me to ask whether she was eligible. I told her she was. Then she asked me how she should fill out the "paper." So I helped her prepare the exemption form. Another mortgagor, who did some extensive remodeling, called to urge me to stop in and see his home improvements. Of course, I made a special trip to inspect his house.

In one case I was bombarded, from both sides, in the financial settlement of a divorce case. The wife was supposed to retain the mortgaged house while the husband was supposed to continue the monthly installments. For several months I received an alternating account of the sins of the other party—but no payments. Since I wasn't particularly worried about any financial loss (the first mortgage was well-seasoned, reduced to a $3,000 balance on a house easily worth $16,000), I could sit back and take an interest in the abominable character of each spouse—as reported by the other. In the end, the divorce lawyers settled the case by arranging to sell the house.

A more affluent homeowner asked for my advice on financing a new swimming pool. Another called to ask me if I thought it would be a good idea if his brother went into debt to lease a filling station. Perhaps the prize case was the tearful wife who called to tell me she was going to lock her husband out of the house and asked me what to do to start divorce action. That quarrel was evidently not as serious as it sounded, for they are still living together on an amicable basis.

I welcome the fact that "my family" is of all colors—white, brown, and black—for I like diversity. And I am looking forward to coming events in my oversized, diverse family—perhaps tomorrow, perhaps next month, perhaps a year from now.

24

WHAT WILL HAPPEN TOMORROW?

Everyone, from the President to the taxi driver, makes economic forecasts. Why shouldn't I? After all, unlike an academic professor of economics, the money I am risking on the basis of my forecast is my own.

● EFFECT OF TIGHT MONEY

This account, which is a record of my actual mortgage investments, goes back to a period when interest rates were much lower than they are today. Even so, my years of mortgage discounting produced a return that doubled my money in six years. The situation today, because of tighter money, would produce much better returns for the investor.

If you were to apply the present money market condition to the mortgage deals presented in this book, you would have to boost every interest rate and every discount that I have mentioned. If a deal identical to the Baker case was negotiated today, the interest rate would be 8½% and the discount would be 45%. The Rivera deal would be a 7% mortgage with a 20% discount. The first 5½% mortgage, at a 4% discount, would be a 6½% mortgage at a 15% discount. That first second mortgage I bought, a 6% mortgage at a 10% discount, would be a 7.2% mortgage at a 25% discount.

I am not presenting these more profitable figures to arouse your cupidity or to urge you to rush into the mortgage discounting business. I am merely demonstrating the effect of changing economic conditions on my business. And I want to suggest, by those altered figures, that the situation can change again—for better or for worse. Let us, therefore, in this added chapter, written at the last moment, try to peer into the future to see what tomorrow will bring.

● INFLATION AND RECESSION

We are living in an unprecedented situation, in an economy that continues to be inflationary while unemployment increases and profit margins drop. There is, in spite of pontifical statements to the contrary, no indication that this general trend will alter drastically. Many of the factors that foster inflation will cease to operate, of course, but the serious underlying problem, the weakening of the American dollar, is not being attacked on the basis of an all-out, coordinated national effort. Serious unemployment, except for minor political moves, seems to be a situation that can actually increase as the national administration continues its enforced withdrawal from an overextended role as world policeman.

What does this projected economic situation mean to the mortgage investor? Inflation, especially at a high rate, has always been a serious problem for mortgage holders and bond holders. When you loan out a fixed number of dollars and get a fixed number of dollars back in the future, the drop in the purchasing power of those returned dollars may be greater than the amount of interest you received during the period of the loan. The ordinary mortgage investor, unless he gets a very high rate of interest, loses. The situation is not so serious for the mortgage discounter, because he invests a small number of dollars and gets a greater number back in the future, thus counteracting the effect of inflation. But even the mortgage discounter, as he views a situation of increasing inflation, should take additional measures to protect himself. He can do this by restricting his purchases to mortgages that have a short-term maturity date. He could, as an added protection, purchase a few well-secured second mortgages on houses in good areas. He would, in these cases, be seriously thinking of acquiring these properties through foreclosure so that he would have an equity position in sound real estate, assets that would become more valuable in terms of a depreciated dollar.

● UNEMPLOYMENT

Unemployment does not have the terrors for the mortgage investor that it once had. There is, as I have mentioned before, a social support for people with financial problems. And I am certain, from the statements of responsible leaders of our political economy, that the moves to counter inflation and strengthen the dollar will be accompanied by the maintenance of a sustenance floor for the urban underprivileged (to forestall riots and revolution, perhaps). This welfare floor means that mortgage payments will continue, even though the homeowner is unemployed.

Let me give you a personal example to illustrate this point. For a number of years, I have held a first mortgage on the home of an older man in a working class district. Married, with four children, he had a steady job in a steel mill. A few years after I bought his mortgage, he began to have serious dizzy spells that made it extremely dangerous for him to work in a place where he was handling glowing ingots of white-hot metal. He stopped working and received unemployment insurance. During this period, he was always behind with his house payments. Finally, the doctors declared him totally disabled. He received a small disability pension and his wife received a monthly check for the care of the children. He immediately became a steady remitter of those payments to me. When his taxes became delinquent, the social welfare worker approved an allotment of money from some special fund to take care of them. I never worry about that mortgage, which now has a balance far below the lowest possible distress sale value of the property.

● URBAN HOUSING PROBLEMS

Because of tight money and high interest rates, there has been an acute shortage of new housing and a restricted market for the sale of homes. During the years 1966 through 1969, there were not quite so many purchase-money mortgages appearing on the market. I thought, at that time, that the supply of mortgages might become so limited that I would not be able to purchase good discount paper—but this period passed. As soon as people became adjusted to the higher rates, they began to buy houses again. And a curious thing happened—more mortgages were offered to private investors. Some of them were first mortgages on lower-priced older houses; many were large second mortgages on good, higher-priced houses.

You can probably see the reason for this. The big savings and loan companies were so short of funds that they would not make loans on second-rate homes. As a result, the only way the seller of such a house could get the money out of his house was to carry back the first mortgage himself and then sell it privately at a discount. As for the good second mortgages, these became more plentiful because institutional first mortgages were being made on a 65% or 70% basis. This loan policy led to down payments beyond the means of many buyers, even though they were receiving higher salaries. To arrange the deal, the seller had to accept a second mortgage to cover the balance of the required down payment. He then sold the second mortgage at a discount.

These recent tendencies convince me that there will be a continuation of an active mortgage market, for we are looking at a primary situation that has been evident for thousands of years. *There will always be people who accumulate money and there will always be people who spend their income as it comes in.* So there will always be savers who can lend their money to those who do not save, and the price of that accommodation is interest that goes to the accumulators. The terms of the exchange may vary, the technique and documents of the lending process may be updated or revised, and the never ending regulation of excesses will always appear—but the return to the prudent saver who keeps abreast of the changing times will always be adequate and the losses inconsequential.

● THE MORTGAGE MARKET WILL ADJUST TO THE MONEY MARKET

Six or seven years ago, when the bank rate for small but responsible borrowers was 6%, I was operating on a scale that was really over my head. I was buying second mortgages on a grand scale (four in one month) and using bank money and private loans to finance my operations. Then the interest rate began to climb, with no appreciable change in mortgage interest rates or discount percentages. I tightened up, paid off my loans, and bought what paper I could handle with my own funds.

But I kept watching the advertised mortgages. I was constantly figuring yields; I watched the price of bonds and the rising cost of loans. At last I saw a definite change in the mortgage market. Rates of interest were higher and discounts were bigger. According to my calculations of yields, it appeared that they had jumped up, on the average, from 12% to 15%. I decided it was time for me to enlarge my activity, for I could now use 9% and 10% bank money on a profitable basis.

In the future, one can operate in the same manner. If the mortgage market fails to follow the money market, sit tight. It will adjust itself upwards through higher discounts. (The mechanism operates, of course, on a two-way stretch. The mortgage buyer, seeing that he can get as much as an 11% yield on a corporation bond, will not buy a mortgage at a low discount. The mortgage seller, unable to raise needed cash from other sources, will agree to a discount that reduces the amount of cash he receives.) If the general interest rates should start down, it might be wise to hurry your purchase of a discounted mortgage so that you can take advantage of the fact that the mortgage market lags behind the general money market.

● GREAT EXPECTATIONS

In the world of politics, as everyone knows, there is a practice of making campaign promises. There is also a tendency by politicians and lawmakers to announce far-reaching social improvements (and even pass a law to bring this about), without authorizing the necessary money to do the job. Time after time, I have seen announcements of housing programs or urban renewal projects or "injection of money" into the housing industry. Each time this happened, I was concerned.

"Now," I said, "the federal government is going to step in and provide the money for decent housing for the working people."

The next month, perhaps, there was another grand announcement of a program that would definitely supply all the money needed for homes.

Shaking my head, I declared, "The government is going to channel billions of dollars through the big savings and loan companies to rebuild everything."

In either case, my position as a small lender to ordinary homeowners was going to be undermined. The private mortgage market would disappear.

But I know better now. The whole thing was a case of fostering great expectations that never came to pass. There will always be houses to be sold to buyers who will pay for them by the now established system of lifelong installment payments, and I will keep right on buying mortgages at a discount. Every morning, as I have in the past, I will be waiting for the mailman to bring those small checks that now add up to a substantial monthly income.

● SOCIAL FORCES MAY CAUSE MAJOR ALTERATION

There is one possibility for the future that seems certain, regardless of the traditional procedures of the past or the oratorical visions of paradise or revolutionary change. Although it moves as slowly as a glacier, it seems equally inexorable and will, I think, produce alterations that could truly be called revolutionary. This is the trend toward multiple housing. This trend, though not consciously planned by politicians or housing industry leaders, seems to be a fact that is, and will be, forced by a combination of many social forces.

There is, first of all, the tremendous population growth in an urbanized society. To house these people in the traditional house-and-yard-per-family milieu requires the use of tremendous areas of land. This, in turn, since new land cannot be produced, forces up the price of what land there is. The people who comprise that increased population will not have the income to pay for expensive housing land used in that wasteful fashion. Houses will squeeze together closer and closer; more apartments will be built, towering higher and higher as the planners seek to accommodate more people per square foot.

There is, also, the tremendous cost of building housing on a single family-per-four-walls basis. These costs are high land prices, as mentioned above, high labor costs, and high financing costs. The American homeowner has fought a good fight against these expenses. He has gone farther and farther away from the city to find a bit of cheap land, sometimes commuting 100 miles daily to and from his job. He has built his own house or bought a small house to which he has added his own additions. He has learned to be a do-it-yourself homeowner. He has tried to circumvent high financing costs by V.A. and other governmental subsidy programs.

But he is fighting a losing battle. Crowded freeways, air pollution, and excessive travel expenses will limit his flight from the city. The building and finance costs are going up faster than his take-home pay, even when his wife works. He will have to give up the battle and retreat to the more economical (per unit) cost of multiple housing.

Another factor is the everlasting rise in taxes on property, which is already resulting in a forced appropriation of the many single-family homes of older people on fixed incomes. There is already a visible movement of the oldest people from their homes to ever-larger convalescent homes for the aged. And those not quite so old are moving to apartments or retirement homes as an intermediate step before they, too, move into the large homes for the aged. (I can show you, not far from my own home, a Hollywood street that has the most extensive building activity in our area. Two large homes for the aged are being built there.) And this tax burden on the single-family home, in spite of various tax relief measures, shows no sign of abatement.

Instead of developing a program of earnest cooperation between the politicians and the multifarious departments of our various local governments to produce the Spartan economy of a bygone day, these servants of the people know but two phrases: "People demand more and more service," and "We must find new tax sources." Such an attitude, if continued, will certainly hasten the destruction of the single-family home.

There has been, more recently, an increase of home robberies, and what is more important, a growing panic, developing at a much greater pace than the actual incidence of theft. This wave of fear is causing a definite tendency for homeowners to abandon their one-family homes and move to the safety of a fenced, lighted, and patrolled multiple housing development.

What does this long-range trend mean to me? It means I must be flexible (perhaps a hard thing for an older man) and prepare for a change of emphasis. Instead of discounting single-family homes, I may invest in apartments, condominiums, and even mobile homes. And you, dear readers, should also be prepared for a whole new range of home investments.

HOW TO USE YIELD TABLES

In order to find the correct yield, you must have four items of information: the rate of interest, the pay-back rate, the time to maturity, and the amount of the discount. The rate of interest and the time to maturity are stated on the promissory note. The amount of the discount (in percentage) is determined by subtracting the price you paid from the remaining principal balance and dividing that potential profit by the principal balance of the mortgage. The pay-back rate, which is the ratio of one monthly payment to the balance of principal, requires another division problem. You divide the principal balance into the monthly payment. Thus, a $20 installment on a $2,000 mortgage is 1; a $15 payment on a $2,000 mortgage is .75; a $25 payment on that $2,000 mortgage would be 1.25; and a $30 payment on that $2,000 mortgage would be 1.50.

Here is a sample problem. You buy a second mortgage with a $3,400 balance. It calls for a monthly payment of $35, including 6% interest. It is all due in five years. You bought it for $2,900, which means that you obtained a 15% discount.

Turn to the 6% Yield Table. Then go down to the section headed "Due in 5 years." Opposite the line marked "15" (on the left) you will find the yields for .75, 1.00, 1.25, and 1.50. Since the note provides for a pay-back rate of approximately 1.00%, you can quickly determine that the yield is 10½%.

Here is another problem. You buy a first mortgage with an $8,000 balance. It calls for a $97.50 monthly installment, including 7½% interest. The note states that payments shall continue "until paid." You obtained it at a price of $7,200, so the discount was 10%.

Turn to the 7.5% Yield Table. At the bottom, you will find the section giving yields for "no due date" maturities. Opposite the line marked "10," you will find your yield. Although the pay-back rate is actually 1.22, the nearest result will be found under the 1.25 heading. Your yield is 10%.

By using these tables on a variety of problems, you will quickly establish that high yields are produced by short maturities, large discounts, and substantial monthly installments. *These three factors are much more important than the interest rates stated on the promissory notes.*

6% Yield Table

Pay-back rates →	.75	1.00	1.25	1.50
Discount ↓		Due in 3 years		
10	10	10¼	10½	10¾
15	12¼	12½	13	13¼
20	14¾	15	15½	16¼
25	17¼	17¾	18½	19¼
30	20	20¾	21½	22½
		Due in 4 years		
10	9¼	9½	9¾	10
15	11	11¼	11¾	12¼
20	12¾	13¼	14	14½
25	14¾	15½	16¼	17¼
30	17	18	19	20
		Due in 5 years		
10	8¾	9	9¼	9½
15	10¼	10½	11	11½
20	11¾	12¼	13	13¾
25	13½	14¼	15	16¼
30	15¼	16¼	17½	18¾
		Due in 6 years		
10	8¼	8½	9	9¼
15	9¾	10	10¾	11¼
20	11	11¾	12½	13½
25	12½	13¼	14¼	15¾
30	14¼	15¼	16½	18¼
		Due in 7 years		
10	8	8½	8¾	pays out
15	9¼	9¾	10½	in less
20	10½	11¼	12	than
25	12	12¾	14	7 years
30	13¼	14½	16	
		Monthly installments until paid (no due date)		
10	7½	8	8¾	9¼
15	8¼	9¼	10¼	11¼
20	9¼	10½	12	13¼
25	10	12	13¾	15½
30	11¼	13½	15¾	18

6.6% Yield Table

Pay-back rates →	.75	1.00	1.25	1.50
Discount ↓		Due in 3 years		
10	10¾	10¾	11	11¼
15	13	13¼	13½	14
20	15¼	15¾	16¼	16¾
25	17¾	18½	19	19¾
30	20½	21¼	22¼	23
		Due in 4 years		
10	9¾	10	10¼	10½
15	11½	12	12¼	12¾
20	13½	14	14½	15¼
25	15½	16	16¾	17¾
30	17½	18½	19½	20½
		Due in 5 years		
10	9¼	9½	9¾	10
15	10¾	11¼	11½	12¼
20	12¼	12¾	13½	14¼
25	14	14¾	15½	16¾
30	15¾	16¾	18	19¼
		Due in 6 years		
10	9	9¼	9½	10
15	10¼	10¾	11¼	12
20	11½	12¼	13	14
25	13	14	15	16¼
30	14¾	15¾	17	18¾
		Due in 7 years		
10	8¾	9	9¼	Pays out
15	9¾	10¼	11	in less
20	11	11¾	12¾	than
25	12½	13¼	14½	7 years
30	14	15	16½	
	Monthly installments until paid (no due date)			
10	8	8¾	9¼	10
15	8¾	9¾	10¾	11¾
20	9½	11	12½	13¾
25	10½	12½	14¼	16
30	11½	14	16¼	18½

7% Yield Table

Pay-back rates →	.75	1.00	1.25	1.50
Discount ↓				
	Due in 3 years			
10	11	11¼	11½	11¾
15	13¼	13½	14	14¼
20	15¾	16	16½	17¼
25	18¼	18¾	19½	20¼
30	21	21¾	22½	23¼
	Due in 4 years			
10	10¼	10½	10¾	11
15	12	12¼	12¾	13¼
20	13¾	14¼	15	15½
25	15¾	16½	17¼	18
30	18	18¾	19¾	21
	Due in 5 years			
10	9¾	10	10¼	10½
15	11⅟	11½	12	12½
20	12¾	13¼	14	14¾
25	14½	15¼	16	17
30	16¼	17¼	18¼	19¾
	Due in 6 years			
10	9¼	9½	10	10¼
15	10½	11	11½	12¼
20	12	12½	13½	14¼
25	13½	14¼	15¼	16½
30	15	16	17½	19
	Due in 7 years			
10	9	9½	9¾	10¼
15	10¼	10¾	11¼	12¼
20	11½	12¼	13	14¼
25	12¾	13¾	14¾	16½
30	14¼	15½	17	19
	Monthly installments until paid (no due date)			
10	8¼	9	9¾	10¼
15	9	10¼	11¼	12¼
20	9¾	11½	12¾	14¼
25	10¾	12¾	14½	16½
30	11¾	14¼	16½	18¾

7.2% Yield Table

Pay-back rates →	.75	1.00	1.25	1.50
Discount ↓		Due in 3 years		
10	11¼	11½	11¾	12
15	13½	13¾	14¼	14½
20	15¾	16¼	16¾	17¼
25	18½	19	19¾	20½
30	21¼	22	22¾	23½
		Due in 4 years		
10	10½	10½	10¾	11¼
15	12¼	12½	13	13¼
20	14	14½	15	15¾
25	16	16¾	17½	18¼
30	18¼	19	20	21¼
		Due in 5 years		
10	9¾	10	10½	10¾
15	11¼	11¾	12¼	12¾
20	13	13½	14	15
25	14½	15¼	16¼	17¼
30	16½	17¼	18½	19¾
		Due in 6 years		
10	9½	9¾	10	10½
15	10¾	11¼	11¾	12½
20	12¼	12¾	13½	14½
25	13¾	14½	15½	16¾
30	15¼	16¼	17½	19¼
		Due in 7 years		
10	9¼	9½	10	10½
15	10½	11	11½	12¼
20	11¾	12¼	13¼	14¼
25	13	14	15	16½
30	14½	15½	17	19
		Monthly installments until paid (no due date)		
10	8½	9¼	9¾	10½
15	9¼	10½	11¼	12¼
20	10	11½	13	14¼
25	11	13	14¾	16½
30	12	14½	16¾	19

7.5% Yield Table

Pay-back rates →	.75	1.00	1.25	1.50
Discount ↓		Due in 3 years		
10	11½	11¾	12	12¼
15	13¾	14	14½	14¾
20	16¼	16½	17	17¾
25	18¾	19¼	20	20¾
30	21½	22¼	23	23½
		Due in 4 years		
10	10¾	11	11¼	11½
15	12½	12¾	13¼	13¾
20	14¼	14¾	15¼	16
25	16¼	17	17¾	18½
30	18½	19¼	20¼	21½
		Due in 5 years		
10	10	10½	10¾	11
15	11½	12	12½	13
20	13¼	13¾	14½	15¼
25	15	15½	16½	17½
30	16¾	17¾	18¾	20
		Due in 6 years		
10	9¾	10	10½	10¾
15	11	11½	12	12¾
20	12½	13	13¾	14¾
25	14	14¾	15¾	17
30	15½	16½	17¾	19½
		Due in 7 years		
10	9½	9¾	10¼	10¾
15	10¾	11¼	11¾	12¾
20	12	12½	13½	14½
25	13¼	14¼	15¼	16¾
30	14¾	15¾	17¼	19¼
	Monthly installments until paid (no due date)			
10	8¾	9½	10	10¾
15	9½	10½	11½	12½
20	10¼	11¾	13¼	14½
25	11¼	13	15	16¾
30	12¼	14½	17	19¼

8% Yield Table

Pay-back rates →	.75	1.00	1.25	1.50
Discount ↓		Due in 3 years		
10	12	12¼	12½	12¾
15	14¼	14½	15	15¼
20	16¾	17	17½	18¼
25	19¼	19¾	20½	21¼
30	22	22¾	23½	24½
		Due in 4 years		
10	11¼	11½	11¾	12
15	13	13¼	13¾	14¼
20	14¾	15¼	15¾	16½
25	16¾	17½	18¼	19
30	19	19¾	20¾	22
		Due in 5 years		
10	10¾	11	11¼	11½
15	12	12½	13	13½
20	13¾	14¼	14¾	15¾
25	15½	16	17	18
30	17¼	18	19¼	20½
		Due in 6 years		
10	10¼	10½	11	11¼
15	11½	12	12½	13¼
20	13	13½	14¼	15¼
25	14½	15¼	16¼	17½
30	16	17	18¼	19¾
		Due in 7 years		
10	10	10¼	10¾	11¼
15	11¼	11¾	12¼	13
20	12½	13	14	15
25	13¾	14¾	15¾	17¼
30	15¼	16¼	17¾	19½
		Monthly installments until paid (no due date)		
10	9¼	10	10½	11¼
15	10	11	12	13
20	10¾	12¼	13½	15
25	11¾	13½	15¼	17¼
30	12½	15	17¼	19½

10% Yield Table

Pay-back rates →	.75	1.00	1.25	1.50
<u>*Discount*</u> ↓		Due in 3 years		
10		14¼	14½	14¾
15		16½	17	17¼
20	No	19	19½	20
25	yield	21¾	22½	23
30	rates	24¾	25½	26½
		Due in 4 years		
10	in	13¼	13½	14
15	this	15¼	15½	16
20	column	17¼	17¾	18½
25	because	19½	20	21
30	a	21¾	22¾	23¾
		Due in 5 years		
10	.75%	12¾	13¼	13½
15	pay-back	14½	15	15½
20	rate	16¼	16¾	17½
25	does	18	18¾	19¾
30	not	20	21	22¼
		Due in 6 years		
10		12½	12¾	13¼
15	cover	14	14½	15
20	the	15½	16¼	17
25	monthly	17	18	19¼
30	interest	19	20	21½
		Due in 7 years		
10		12¼	12¾	13
15		13½	14¼	14¾
20		15	15¾	16¾
25		16½	17½	18¾
30		18¼	19½	21
		Monthly installments until paid (no due date)		
10		11¾	12½	13
15		12¾	13¾	14¾
20		13¾	15¼	16¾
25		15	16¾	18¾
30		16¼	18¾	21

INDEX